BARNES & NOBLE BASICS™
volunteering

by Hope Egan

BARNES
&NOBLE
BOOKS

For information, contact:
Silver Lining Books
122 Fifth Avenue
New York, NY 10011
212-633-4000

Titles in the **Barnes & Noble Basics**™ series:
Barnes & Noble Basics *Getting a Grant*

introduction

How can I help? It's a question that says a lot about you. It says that you care, that you are compassionate, that you want to make a difference. The problem, if there is one, is where to start. You want to help. But how? Where? When?

The answers to these questions are right here in **Barnes & Noble Basics** *Volunteering*. It walks you through the entire volunteer world. *Volunteering* describes the wide range of organizations that welcome help, such as fire-fighting groups, garden clubs, political parties, disaster relief organizations, children's hospitals, literacy groups, wildlife organizations, and many more. In addition to describing the organizations, each chapter looks at their key volunteer activities. Are you interested in helping the homeless? Check out pages 98–99. Want to help improve education in your school district? Then consider the PTA or running for the Board of Education—two organizations run solely by volunteers. Ever dreamed of volunteering abroad? Then see pages 174–193. There's a whole world of volunteering out there waiting for you.

Barb Chintz
Editorial Director, the **Barnes & Noble Basics**™ series

table of contents

1

Getting started

Many volunteers sign up to give, but they end up receiving much more than they ever imagined.

why volunteer?

Most people start volunteering because they want to spend time and energy for a cause that they believe in, contribute to their community or country, and help others. But many volunteers report that although they signed up to give, they ended up receiving much more than they ever imagined. Read on and see how volunteering can change you and the world around you for the better.

Reasons to Be a Volunteer

- Meet new people.
- Make new friends.
- Learn about social issues.
- Interact with people who share your interests and passions.
- Network in your current line of work.
- Develop new skills and talents for your resumé.
- Change career directions.
- Maintain your skills during a period of layoff.
- Improve your knowledge about a particular topic.
- Dust off skills that have been dormant for a while.
- Get training that will benefit you later.
- Develop a new hobby.
- Make a unique contribution—that is, make something happen that wouldn't have been possible without you.
- Get satisfaction by knowing you're doing good work well—and have fun in the process.

ASK THE EXPERTS

Can volunteering help my career?

Sure! While the main motivator for volunteering should be your desire to make a difference, you might be surprised at the number of ways volunteering can boost your career: You can fine-tune or gain skills that can help you get a raise or a promotion. For example, supervising other volunteers might help you move into your first management position. The heightened self-esteem and satisfaction you derive from volunteering spills over into your attitude and enthusiasm at work. You might develop business contacts that will open important doors for you in the future—and you just might meet someone who wants to hire you (or use your employer's services) after seeing you in action and observing your dedication and selfless hard work.

Is volunteering a good way to meet my potential mate?

Absolutely. Not only will you be giving your time to a good cause, but you'll be meeting other like-minded people who may be generous, giving, and have compassion for others. And since volunteers often work side-by-side, it's an ideal way to get to know someone's character, interests, and quirks without the pressures of blind dates or singles ads.

TURNING POINT

When my friend Ruth asked me to join the board of directors of an organization that honors heroes of the civil rights movement, I was nervous about what I was getting myself into. Although I had some writing and public relations experience, I was an accountant by trade. The board already had a treasurer, however, and I was thrust into the position of public relations expert. While I didn't think I knew that much about PR, I found I was a fast learner. In fact, before long, my story pitch about our project attracted a reporter who wrote an article on the front of the metro section of our local newspaper! I found PR so exciting that I took several classes in it, and now it's my full-time job.

—Sarah F., Chicago, Illinois

who needs help?

The world of nonprofits

As you prepare to volunteer, the natural question to ask is, "Who needs my help?" The list is endless—every school, church, synagogue, museum, and most hospitals, to name but a few. The most common way to donate your time is through a nonprofit organization. A **nonprofit** is any institution (school, hospital, foundation) created to accomplish some charitable, humanitarian, or educational purpose. Because nonprofits aren't in the business of creating wealth, they generally don't have to pay any corporate income tax on money they make. Likewise, donations to nonprofits are usually tax-deductible for the donor.

VolunteerMatch offers you countless opportunities to do good, such as finding homes for abandoned cats.

Nonprofits span the full range of interests and concerns. They may be involved in religious, educational, scientific, or literary pursuits. They may advance the cause of amateur sports, the prevention of cruelty to children or animals, relief for the poor, or work to combat discrimination, community deterioration, or juvenile delinquency. Still other nonprofits take the form of political or lobbying organizations, social clubs, and unions.

Almost all nonprofits depend heavily on private donations, government funding, and **grants** (money given by a government agency or a foundation) to cover their expenses. (For more on grants see pages 206–207.) There is tremendous competition among nonprofits for these funds. Nonprofit budgets are often in the red, and many operate on a shoestring. In fact, the single biggest expense for many nonprofits is staff salary—so most depend on volunteers just to stay in business.

The bottom line? The more volunteers nonprofits can enlist, the more they can accomplish.

ASK THE EXPERTS

With so many volunteer opportunities out there, where do I turn to find one?

There are a couple of different routes you can take. If you know which organization you want to volunteer for (whether or not you know what type of work you want to do), call them. Many larger nonprofits have a **volunteer coordinator**—a full-time staff person dedicated to helping volunteers find a good fit within their organization. What if they don't have a volunteer coordinator? No problem—be a self-starter and ask the person who answers the phone how you can help.

How can I find out more?

For a taste of volunteering before you commit to a particular group or cause, check out City Cares at 404-875-7334 or **www.citycares.org.** Located in more than 30 major cities, City Cares is a great way to get involved if you're not sure what you want to do or if you're looking for a short-term commitment. Also, the Points of Light Foundation (**www.pointsoflight.org**) sponsors a variety of annual one-time service opportunities, including Make a Difference Day (the fourth Saturday of October) and Martin Luther King Day (in January). You can also contact your nearest United Way by clicking to **www.unitedway.org** or checking your local white pages for a listing. Or visit **www.volunteermatch.org** or **www.usafreedomcorps.gov**—two of the best Internet resources for finding local volunteer opportunities. Finally, most churches and synagogues should be able to connect you with local volunteer opportunities.

Are there both front- and back-office types of volunteer positions?

Yes. Behind-the-scenes work, which is common to all nonprofits, includes administrative and promotional roles that help raise money and awareness, and keep the organization running. These are covered in the next chapter. The hands-on work is the nitty-gritty services that the organization is set up to do. This might include teaching a health seminar or operating a soup kitchen, for example. You'll find information about these volunteer opportunities peppered throughout the rest of this book.

finding a fit

What volunteer work is right for you?

Deciding to volunteer is a big first step. Doing the legwork to make sure you're volunteering at the right place, in the right position, and for the right reasons, should be your next task. By making sure you have a good fit, you'll not only gain satisfaction from your experience, you'll also do the most good.

unidos por los niños del mundo

You can deliver food, toys, and smiles through Kiwanis clubs in the United States and abroad (for example, in El Salvador, as shown here). In any language, the goal of Kiwanis clubs is the same: serving the children of the world.

You won't have to figure out all of this completely on your own. Most large nonprofits have people whose job is to make sure that volunteers are placed in positions that are appropriate for them. Here are some questions to ponder.

■ **How do you feel about the organization's mission?** By perusing their Web site and brochures and talking to their current employees, you can get a feel for the organization's mission. How does its mission fit with yours? While they don't have to match up exactly, it's important that they be compatible.

■ **What's your motivation?** People often feel the urge to volunteer because of past experiences and what they have witnessed. For example, people who have felt the warmth of a hospice worker when their parent was dying might want to be a hospice volunteer. Or if you know someone suffering from Alzheimer's disease, you might want to help raise money to find a cure.

■ **What are all of the volunteer positions the organization has available?** You might have approached a particular organization (Big Brothers Big Sisters of America, for example) because you felt passionately about their cause (children), but its primary volunteer opportunity (mentoring) may not be the best fit for you. Don't be afraid to seek out less visible volunteer opportunities. Maybe you're a lawyer who wants to review the organization's lease agreements or a graphic designer who wants to improve its newsletter. Call or write the supervisors of these areas and offer to help.

- **How does the organization view its volunteers?** In some cases, volunteers do the same work as paid staff, are treated the same, and basically fold right into the culture. Other organizations clearly delineate volunteers from staff by creating volunteer newsletters or recognition awards. Talk to other volunteers about their experiences—and to the nonprofit's employees as well—to find out what the volunteer culture is like.

- **What will the organization expect of you?** Just as you wouldn't accept a paid job without knowing what your employer expected of you, you'll want to be clear what the expectations are for your volunteer position before you accept it.

ASK THE EXPERTS

Are background checks common?

Yes. Many organizations—especially if they deal with such vulnerable groups as children, the disabled, or the elderly—will require you to submit to a routine background check. Don't worry: They're not looking for every "youthful indiscretion" you might have committed. Instead, they generally screen for people who might pose a real threat to the people being cared for. To help out the charity and to illustrate your commitment, you might be asked to pick up the tab for the background check, which could run from $10 to $40. While the process might be a slight inconvenience, don't let it discourage you from taking the leap.

How can I get along with a difficult volunteer supervisor?

Like the business world, the nonprofit world is full of conflicting personalities. As you would in a paid job, try to talk to the person. If she is quick to anger, make sure you understand what she's asked you to do; maybe there's simply been a miscommunication that you're not aware of. Or maybe she's overworked and needs your help even more than you realize. If a talk doesn't help, ask the volunteer coordinator if you can be reassigned.

managing expectations

What they expect—and what you should

An organization's nonprofit status doesn't mean that it isn't professional and businesslike—and a good nonprofit will expect the same of its volunteers. Besides, if an organization puts time and resources into screening, training, and fitting you into a volunteer slot, it has every right to expect that your attitude and commitment will mirror those of its employees.

Try to adjust your thinking so that you don't show up with an "I'm doing you a favor" attitude. You should adhere to the organization's guidelines for behavior, dress appropriately, and have a good attitude. (Sometimes just having a cheerful face in the midst of a stressful environment can be helpful.)

While most nonprofits are very businesslike, others are not. If you're frustrated because you think the organization could be doing things better, relax, take a deep breath, and try to find out the reasoning behind their methods. Know what you're talking about before you rush to share your "business insights."

If you arrive at the conclusion that you could indeed help improve business practices, ask the executive director if your suggestions would be welcome. If the answer is yes, go for it!

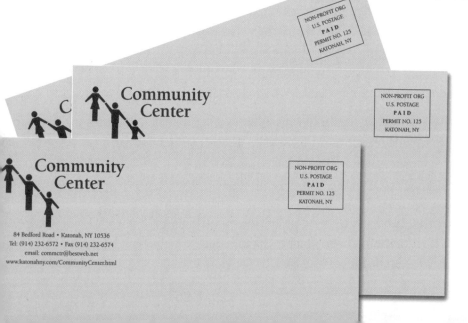

What to Expect, as a Volunteer, From a Large Organization

■ A response to your application, whether you applied by phone or mail, generally comes within 30 days.

■ Written job descriptions exist for all volunteer positions.

■ Standard orientation sessions are held to show all new volunteers the ropes.

■ Training is provided as necessary.

■ Volunteers are given feedback about their work and recognition for their efforts.

What a Volunteer Organization Expects From You

■ Arrive on time.

■ Understand the organization's goals and objectives.

■ Fulfill your promises and commitments to others in the organization.

■ Give an evaluation of the organization and its program so it can learn and improve its service to the community and other volunteers.

■ Respect the rights of all parties in the organization.

What Is Your Compatibility?

Here are some questions to ask yourself to see how compatible you are with different volunteer groups.

■ **Time** How much time do I have to give?

■ **Skills and resources** What special talents or connections do I have in this field?

■ **Money and fund-raising** How comfortable am I with raising money?

■ **People skills** Do I like to work with people?

■ **Work style** Do I like to work alone or in a group?

Use your preferences to help you decide what volunteer roles and organizations best suit you.

family volunteering

Working together

If you want to volunteer but are concerned about shrinking the already dwindling time you spend with your family, consider asking them to participate. Because nonprofits know that allowing families to volunteer will help them get more warm bodies working on a project, some actually encourage the practice!

What is a "family" composed of? Sometimes it's the whole family—both parents and every child. It could also be only a husband and wife or maybe a parent and child who welcome volunteering as a bonding experience. Maybe it's a single parent and her kids, or even just the children on their own. Whatever the configuration, family members who volunteer can share meaningful time together while contributing to a worthy cause—and can gain new and deeper topics for conversation around the dinner table.

How should a family decide where to volunteer? It's important that all members feel they've been part of the decision-making process, so set aside time to talk about each person's major societal concerns. Popular projects for families include providing food for the hungry, teaching literacy, visiting or helping the elderly, and cleaning up the environment. Try brainstorming ideas for volunteer projects and for potential organizations that might need your help. Then have one family member do research on your options before you decide.

After volunteering, make sure to take time to discuss the project. Ask questions about other family members' experiences, feelings, and observations—and be ready to share yours.

Working together with your family helps instill the volunteer spirit in your child. Here, a mom and her son gather school supplies to give to underprivileged students.

ASK THE EXPERTS

How can I find family-friendly volunteer opportunities?

Some large employers—including Carnival Cruise Lines, Target, Motorola, Sears, and Allstate—encourage their employees to volunteer with their families so that they don't have to sacrifice quality time with their loved ones. You can also visit **www.volunteermatch.com** for opportunities; volunteer positions marked with a small brown G are good for group volunteering, while ones with a pink K are appropriate for kids.

What if my family "bites off more than it can chew" with a project?

Try to keep your volunteer supervisor informed of any changes or disruptions that can affect your family commitment. Planning ahead and being honest with yourself before making the commitment is the best way to avoid breaking it. If a problem does occur, remember that volunteer families can often enlist the help of other volunteers to pick up the slack.

What if it turns out that the organization is set up more for individuals than for groups?

Know when to move on, but don't be afraid to get creative. Consider grouping similar tasks or requirements together and assigning different responsibilities to each family member. If, for example, an organization needs help with mail delivery, answering phones, and writing thank-you notes, work with the volunteer coordinator to create an "administration" position for each task.

donating goods

Your extra stuff may be just what they need

Charities don't just need volunteer services; they also need goods. If you'd like to help certain groups, consider giving away your stuff—you'll not only be contributing to a good cause but will get a tax deduction in the process.

Many organizations will accept your household items. Whether you want to get rid of clothes your children have outgrown or furniture and appliances you've grown tired of, there's probably an organization out there somewhere that needs them.

Some rules about donating goods: Make sure that anything you donate is in good condition—if the organization can't resell the item, they don't want to be burdened with the cost of disposing of it. Also consider that organizations that give away goods want to maintain their clients' dignity by offering them items that are in reasonably good shape.

Next, because donations to charitable organizations are often tax-deductible, make sure they give you a receipt; it will be up to you and your accountant to make an honest estimate of your donation's value. Finally, keep in mind that while some charities will pick up items from your home, rising costs are making this once standard service less and less common.

One more thing: If you have time to volunteer for charities, remember that they need people to sort through all this stuff!

Who Needs What?

Donations to the Salvation Army (consult **www.salvationarmy.org** or check your local phone book) are sold in its thrift stores. The proceeds are used to support the organization's rehabilitation centers, which help destitute people get back on their feet. A variety of volunteer opportunities exist with the group: Bell-ringers are needed for Christmastime kettles, thrift stores need clerks and people to sort clothes, and food pantries need supervisors and stockers. To get involved, contact your local Salvation Army center and ask for the officer in charge.

Goodwill Industries (**www.goodwill.org** or 800-664-6577) uses donated clothes and household goods to raise money for people with disabilities and other special needs, and provides them with job training and placement.

You can donate just about anything else as well, if you look hard enough for someone who needs it. That includes used cars (try **www.carshelpingpeople.org** or **www.donateacar.com**); eyeglasses (contact Lions Clubs at **www.lionsclubs.org**); and computers (click to Share the Technology, **www.sharetechnology.org**).

ⒶSK THE EXPERTS

What are the tax consequences of giving away my stuff?

Donating goods is like getting paid to do spring cleaning: The IRS lets you deduct the fair market value of anything you donate to charity. (While a charity should give you a receipt for these donations, it's you, not the charity, who decides what dollar value to assign to it.) But how do you know what fair market value is? In some case, it's pretty simple. For example, if you donate stock, you can use the figures published in the newspaper on the day of your donation. For clothing, furniture, and other household goods, the fair market value is how much a thrift store might charge for the same items, in the same condition. But if you donate a car, beware! While the Blue Book value might give you clues to your auto's fair value, you need to factor in any repairs that are needed and can claim only how much you could—realistically—have sold it for.

donating funds

Open up your wallet—and your heart

For any nonprofit, there are always some things that only money can buy: rent, utilities, transportation costs, and staff and volunteer training costs. So if you're getting cold feet about giving your time to a certain cause, or have decided to volunteer somewhere else, you should still think about writing a check.

How much should you give? There's no right answer; every penny really does count. If you can't afford much, just give what you're comfortable with. For example, even if the "suggested donation" is $50, most charities are happy to accept your $5. Some employers have matching-gift programs, meaning they'll match your donations to the groups that you choose. Ask your human resources department for details. You also might get a tax deduction by giving money, provided you have enough deductions to itemize your return.

Don't get hustled; check out prospective charities to make sure they're on the up-and-up. Call the Better Business Bureau Wise Giving Alliance at 703-276-0100 or click to **www.give.org**, **www.guidestar.org**, or **www.charitywatch.org**.

ASK THE EXPERTS

Can I deduct money I give for political causes?

No. Even though political organizations, labor unions, and social clubs might technically be nonprofit organizations, donations to them are generally not deductible.

Is the money I give to buy Girl Scout cookies tax-deductible?

Not really. In general, when you get something in return for a payment to a charity—even a box of cookies that's gobbled up on the spot—only the amount in excess of the item's value is tax-deductible.

now what do I do?
Answers to common questions

The September 11 attacks on America really jump-started my desire to volunteer. Short of joining the Army, is there any way I can help our country?

Yes! As a response to this tragedy, President Bush called upon all Americans to volunteer. The newly created Citizen Corps provides a way for citizens to help prevent and respond to terrorism, crime, and other disasters. Through Citizen Corps you can be part of a Community Emergency Response Team that responds to disasters; join in community policing (Volunteers in Police Service); join a council to help develop your community's programs and plans (Citizen Corps Councils); and help healthcare professionals during large-scale emergencies (Medical Reserve Corps). You can also get involved as part of the USA Freedom Corps (which includes the Peace Corps, AmeriCorps, and SeniorCorps). For more information, check **www.citizencorps.gov**, call your local mayor's office, or e-mail askcitizencorps@citizencorps.gov.

I feel funny calling up and asking to volunteer. How do most people get started?

Most volunteers started simply because someone asked for help. If no one gets around to asking and you are shy about making that call, actively make yourself available. Many volunteer positions are posted on nonprofit Web sites. Look for one that appeals to you and send an e-mail. If you are uncomfortable with this, attend local charity functions where there may be a call for volunteers or where someone may specifically request your help.

I'd like to volunteer, but I'm so pressed for time that I don't think I can make a real difference.

You're smart not to overcommit yourself. But if you really do want to help out, consider Virtual Volunteering. Online volunteering can take many forms: You can tutor or mentor a child via e-mail; perform writing, editing, or database management work from your computer; or design or maintain a nonprofit's Web site. Visit **www.volunteermatch.org** or **www.usafreedomcorps.gov** to find these opportunities. For still more information about Virtual Volunteering, click to **www.serviceleader.org/vv/**.

What is a volunteer center?

These are clearinghouses that match volunteers with local community service opportunities. They vary in size. In some cities there is only one part-time employee; other cities have large organizations with 40 full-time employees or more. These centers are either stand-alone nonprofits or a part of an independent nonprofit, like the United Way. To find the nearest volunteer center, call the Points of Light Foundation at 800-865-8683, or visit **www.volunteerconnections.org**.

Now where do I go?

CONTACTS

City Cares
404-875-7334
www.citycares.org
An alliance of volunteer organizations working to build community through service and civic engagement.

The Points of Light Foundation and National Volunteer Center Network
800-865-8683
www.volunteerconnections.org

United Way
www.unitedway.org

Volunteer Match
www.volunteermatch.org
One of the best Internet resources for finding local volunteer opportunities.

Catholic Charities
703-549-1390
www.catholiccharitiesusa.org
Encompasses more than 1,400 local agencies and institutions—and you don't have to be Catholic to help.

The Red Cross
www.redcross.org

YMCA
800-872-9622
www.ymca.net

USA FreedomCorps
www.usafreedomcorps.gov
The government's new comprehensive clearinghouse helps individuals find local volunteer opportunities.

Network for Good
www.networkforgood.org

BOOKS

The Kid's Guide to Service Projects: Over 500 Service Ideas for Young People Who Want to Make a Difference
By Barbara A. Lewis and Pamela Espeland

Family Serve:
Volunteer Opportunities for Families
By Mary Thoele

From Making a Profit to Making a Difference: How to Launch Your New Career in Nonprofits
By Richard M. King

Chicken Soup for the Volunteer's Soul
By Jack Canfield, Mark Victor Hansen (Editor), Arline McGraw Oberst, John T. Boal, Tom and Laura Lagana

Reflections for the Effective Nonprofit Volunteer: Quotes, Axioms and Observations to Help You Serve Our Important Institutions
By Jim Norvell

2
What can I do?

Share your skills, learn new ones, or just be there for those in need.

skills you can use

Tasks for the talented — and those who want to learn

So you're ready to start volunteering? Great! But what exactly do you want to do? While many volunteer positions don't require special skills or training, most nonprofits want to benefit from any skill or interest you already have or want to develop.

Nonprofits have the same needs as any for-profit business. People are enlisted to answer the phones, keep track of the money, maintain the Web site, design brochures, render legal services, sit on the board of directors, and plan annual events. Then, of course, there is the direct work they do, whether organizing food drives or fund-raisers, or caring for animals in the zoo.

Typical Volunteer Jobs

Here are the types of volunteer positions you may find at nonprofit groups ranging from your profession's trade association to your community's food bank.

President Organize and run meetings; act as a clearinghouse for all publicity, correspondence, and planning.

Vice president Act as backup to the president; coordinate and prepare for folder-stuffing meeting.

Recording secretary Record minutes and mail; send out reminder postcards for meetings.

Corresponding secretary Send out thank-you notes; committee recognition.

Treasurer Pay bills, prepare a simple budget.

Publicity Proofread brochure; send press releases to four local papers and school newsletters.

Building management Submit building-use forms; coordinate scheduling of time or bus transportation for students.

Brochure Lay out brochure and submit to the president; send wording of workshop to each speaker for O.K.

Food Arrange for and coordinate food and beverages for the fund-raiser with the caterer.

Most likely, this hands-on work for a good cause is what interests you most. But don't forget about the many behind-the-scenes tasks that have to be taken care of before that work can be done. Many organizations need more volunteer help in these administrative areas than they do with hands-on jobs.

ASK THE EXPERTS

Is it smart to volunteer the same skill that I use at work?

It depends. Do some soul-searching before you volunteer in the same capacity as your full-time job. You might crunch numbers during the day, but that doesn't mean doing the books for a charity will prove satisfying. Many folks get the most enjoyment from donating skills that don't otherwise get used.

The local food pantry's Web site is a mess. I'm a professional programmer, so should I volunteer to help fix it?

If you see an area that needs help, volunteer to fix it. Charities need—and rely upon—people to donate their vocational skills. But because each group has its own priorities, don't feel bad if they pass on the offer.

I've just graduated from beauty school and want to use my new skills for a good cause. Any suggestions?

Look Good . . . Feel Better (**www.lookgoodfeelbetter.org**) is a national program that teaches beauty techniques to women who are fighting cancer. The program helps these women restore their self-image and cope with effects that cancer treatment has on their appearance. If you want to provide cosmetology services to homeless or abused women, simply contact a local homeless or domestic violence shelter. Even if they don't have a formal volunteer program, they'll probably find a way to use your services.

No Skills? No Problem!

If you're drawn to a particular position—say, tagging butterflies caught in the wild—but don't have the skills for it, don't give up. Depending on the organization, the skill, and the commitment you're willing to make, many nonprofits will provide you with on-the-job training. You'll not only be able to learn a new skill, you'll also see how interested you are in pursuing the activity as a vocation.

leadership skills

Becoming a leader takes practice

Some leaders are born—but most of the rest of us have to work at it. The good news: If you've never led a group and want to develop your leadership skills, volunteering is a great place to start. Why? Because leaders are always needed to head volunteer projects, committees, boards, and events. Opportunities abound.

What exactly do volunteer leaders do? Their primary function is to act as the person who stays above the fray and clearly directs the project to a successful and happy completion. Good leaders know how to build a consensus and find who can bring which skills to the volunteer table. In short, a leader makes things happen. Most volunteer leaders are also the people who are most heavily involved in their community. As the saying goes, "If you want something done, give it to a busy person." Nowhere is this more true than in volunteering.

If the idea of leading a volunteer project feels daunting, don't panic. You can do it!

ASK THE EXPERTS

I was asked to lead my company's United Way program this year, but I have no experience of that kind. What if I screw up?

The good thing about volunteering is that the criteria for success and failure are different from those of the for-profit world. In the latter, a healthy bottom line is considered the hallmark of success. In the nonprofit world, a large turnout to an event, a renewed interest in a cause, and even a slight increase in funds raised are all reasons to celebrate. As a leader of a volunteer project, you may be surprised to find how easy it is to use your social and organizational skills. If you still have doubts, ask for advice from others who have led similar volunteer efforts.

What if those I'm leading have more leadership experience that I do?

Leading leaders can be tricky, particularly because every leader has his or her own style. The most important trait you can exhibit is good communication. Make sure people know where things are going, how they fit, and what success looks like. Then add a dash of humility, and you and your team will be on the right path.

fund-raising and development

Finding funds and financial support

Most nonprofits would probably list fund-raising as their most desperate need. That's because, like any corporation, they are saddled with telephone, electricity, and similar costs—not to mention the staff members' salaries. But unlike for-profit corporations, most charities and nonprofits are not "selling" anything—in fact, nonprofits are in the business of *giving away* money, time, and effort. To help keep themselves operational, they turn to fund-raising.

Fund-raising can take many different forms, so don't rule it out just because you're not a naturally gifted salesperson. Much important fund-raising is done by taking advantage of relationships you already have. Perhaps you'll have to find corporate sponsors for a silent auction or a golf outing. Or you may join the capital campaign for raising money for your church or synagogue's new building. You can also sign on to help with **event planning**—the planning and staging of a major fund-raising event (for more on that, see page 36).

Getting a Grant

If you're a writer and want to help with fund-raising, try your hand at writing a grant proposal. Most charities use grants to fund special projects and programs. Similar to a business plan, a typical proposal describes the project and the problems it will solve, outlines how the organization plans to solve them, and what costs will be incurred (for more on grants, see pages 206–207). If you don't have experience with grants but are interested in learning, check out **Barnes & Noble Basics** *Getting a Grant*.

ASK THE EXPERTS

Are there any one-time opportunities to volunteer that can give me an idea about whether fund-raising work suits me?

Are there ever! The best way to check out a charity—and help them in their greatest area of need—is to volunteer for their annual fund-raiser. Often the single biggest source of revenue, fund-raisers need sales-oriented people to help with all of the typical fund-raising chores: selling tickets to an event, securing corporate sponsors, and getting food and other items donated. For other fund-raising ideas, see pages 36–37.

I want to help raise money for my local homeless shelter, but I'm not really a salesperson. Can I still help?

Definitely. Most fund-raising opportunities require a variety of skills that have nothing to do with "selling." By volunteering to maintain its database or Web site, stuff envelopes for a solicitation letter, or raise awareness of the shelter's presence, you'll still be contributing to the shelter's fund-raising efforts.

How do I get over my feelings of fear and embarrassment when asking friends or strangers for money?

We often feel that asking for money somehow offends the people we're asking. Most of all, we fear they'll say no. Just make clear why you're soliciting a donation and be specific about how the funds will benefit the organization. The more donors know, the more they're likely to contribute. And if they don't? Simply move on to another prospective donor.

communications and publicity

Getting the word out

No matter how righteous your cause, you've got to work hard to get the word out. Raising awareness not only spreads the group's message but also helps it raise money and recruit more volunteers—two things crucial to accomplishing its goals.

People and corporations are much more likely to donate to a cause once they've read about it in the newspaper, heard about it on the radio, or received periodic newsletters. Getting the word out is also important for finding new volunteers.

There are usually ample opportunities to serve in this capacity—whether you have any experience or not. Send out press releases and call local newspapers, magazines, and TV and radio stations about upcoming events. Pin flyers on bulletin boards. Hang posters at local businesses. In short, do whatever's necessary to get the message heard.

ASK THE EXPERTS

I'm not sure I could make phone calls to the press or plan a fund-raiser, but I'm a whiz with words. Do most groups need writing help?

Yes! Like any other organization, a nonprofit produces tons of printed materials, including mailings, press releases, and perhaps an annual report. But don't overlook other possibilities, such as editing the quarterly volunteer newsletter, creating content for their Web site, or even churning out handwritten thank-you letters to donors.

I'm good at graphic design. Do most groups need help with it?

In general, the larger the group, the more likely graphic design will be handled by professionals. But most small nonprofits *do* need design help. Don't overlook one-time opportunities—say, designing Bowl-a-Thon T-shirts or the invitations to the New Year's Eve fund-raiser. Who knows? You might end up designing the organization's logo.

I've always wanted to be a photographer, but my portfolio is still a little weak. Where can I volunteer to get more experience?

You'd be surprised how many opportunities exist for volunteer photographers. For example, any organization that produces a newsletter could probably use someone to shoot pictures of their annual fund-raising dinner or other special events. Some environmental organizations (parks, forests, botanical gardens) want photographers to photograph their collections for their Web site or a newsletter. And your local theater might want photographs taken of their actors—both head shots and action shots.

advocacy

Bringing the message home

Many groups make it their goal to influence public opinion and government policy on crucial issues. This they do through letter-writing campaigns, individual meetings with government officials, and, sometimes, mass demonstrations.

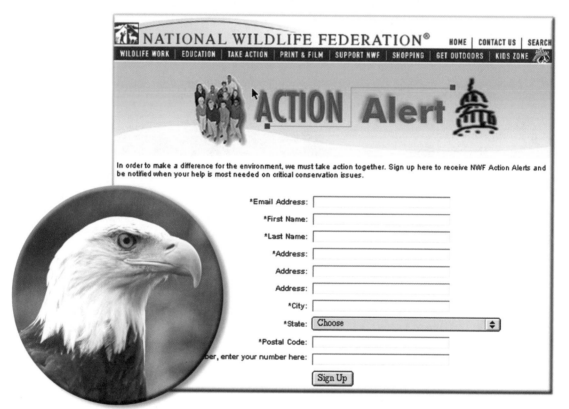

Make a difference for the environment through the National Wildlife Federation. Write letters or send e-mail to Congress, or organize a neighborhood fund-raiser.

If the issue you're passionate about is mainstream, chances are good that there's already a large organization working to support your cause. If you're concerned about global human rights, contact Amnesty International; for wildlife advocacy, contact the National Wildlife Federation; for the homeless, contact the National Coalition for the Homeless; for the environment, contact the Sierra Club. You get the picture.

You may already be donating money to a group of this kind (or enjoying the benefits of their work, whether you realize it or not). Now is the time to get involved with the group of your choice.

Ask the Experts

What do advocacy groups want from me?

Once you've found the appropriate organization—and depending on your interests, availability, and skills—you'll be asked to help with general office duties, fund-raising, influencing decision-makers, and raising public awareness about your issue. This may mean voting like-minded politicians into office or contacting your representative in Congress. But you may simply be asked to staff a booth at the local mall, to sign a petition, or to be part of the speaker's bureau that travels to schools, senior homes, or community events to raise awareness for your cause or organization.

Advocacy Groups

■ **Amnesty International** Promotes worldwide human rights by helping to free prisoners of conscience; ensuring fair trials for political prisoners; and striving to end the death penalty, torture, and other cruel treatment of prisoners.
www.amnesty.org (worldwide) or **www.aiusa.org** (USA) 212-807-8400 or e-mail admin-us@aiusa.org

■ **National Wildlife Federation** Educational organization that brings together individuals, organizations, businesses, and government to protect wildlife, natural resources, and the environment. **www.nwf.org** 800-822-9919

■ **National Coalition for the Homeless** Uses public education and advocacy to help end homelessness. **www.nationalhomeless.org** 202-737-6444 or e-mail info@nationalhomeless.org

■ **Mothers Against Drunk Driving** Looks for solutions to the drunk driving and underage drinking problems. **www.madd.org** 800-438-6233

■ **ACORN (Association of Community Organizations for Reform Now)** Addresses issues for low- and moderate-income families, such as first-time home buying and tenant issues, living wages for low-wage workers, increased community investment from banks and governments, and better public schools.
www.acorn.org

---

event planning

Putting all the
pieces together

Most nonprofit organizations hold special events as fund-raisers. These could be holiday parties or the twice-yearly clean-up-the-park day. These special activities require event planning—in other words, organization. In large charity organizations, a staff person or paid consultant usually organizes the whole thing and then seeks dozens of volunteers to help plan the event or simply to help out on the day of the grand affair.

If you're new to event planning, don't worry—they won't make you run things. Depending on your skills, you might be asked to help scout out a location for the shindig, talk to caterers about their prices and menus, or help the decorating committee. Working with the publicity people is important too, in order to make sure the word gets out—and people show up!

On the other hand, small organizations that are planning to hold a fund-raising event may need a leader to step forward. If you're organized, detail-oriented, and love to give parties, maybe that leader should be you.

ASK THE EXPERTS

How can I get started doing event planning?

Once you know which organization you'd like to volunteer for, ask their volunteer coordinator if they have any event-planning needs. If they don't have a volunteer coordinator, get in touch with people in development (another word for fund-raising).

Are there any one-time opportunities to help with events?

Fund-raisers and other events are the best time to jump in and get a feel for volunteering. You can often sign up to help on that day only. "Set-up" volunteers arrange chairs, set the tables, and light candles to prepare for the party. When guests arrive, other volunteers greet them, take their tickets, or hand out programs. Some functions need volunteers to serve the meals. And cleanup volunteers? Well, you know what they do.

I enjoy arranging get-togethers and welcoming people, but I'm looking for an ongoing opportunity on a smaller scale. What can I do?

Many organizations need to line up hospitality experts for their regular gatherings. For example, your local synagogue might use volunteer members to organize and prepare for their weekly Oneg Shabbat (Joy of the Sabbath) gatherings. Your local church might have a hospitality team that welcomes visitors on Sundays and arranges to serve coffee and muffins to encourage people to mingle after services. Homeless shelters and hospitals are other examples of organizations that often need volunteers to welcome tired, scared, or vulnerable visitors.

computer skills

Computer technology and the Internet have become essential to doing business. But the cost of hiring information technology professionals is sky-high, so nonprofits often rely on volunteers for crucial technology-related tasks. The variety of ongoing and project-oriented work is endless. And depending on the project you choose, you might be able to work remotely.

If you are an information technology professional (or have significant IT skills), volunteer opportunities abound. Create or upgrade your favorite museum's Web site. Or design or maintain the food pantry's mailing database.

If you enjoy computers but don't know Java from a cup of coffee, you might still find a volunteer position that requires only the most basic computer skills. For example, you can mentor the elderly or youths who are learning to use the computer and Internet. Or help keep the PTA's Web site up to date with announcements or event information.

TURNING POINT

After my daughter and granddaughter were killed in a car accident, I became severely depressed and nearly reclusive. One day I felt so out of touch with the world that I knew I had to do something. So I made a rare trip out and went to the local bookstore. Of all things, I picked up a book on Web design, took it home, and found myself reading it and dabbling with the design process on my computer. A concerned friend told me about a support group for bereaved parents and suggested that I volunteer for them to lift my spirits, so I offered to try my hand at designing a Web site for our local chapter. I did, and they were very appreciative. The whole process helped me work my way out of my depression.

— **Martha H., Sioux City, Iowa**

ASK THE EXPERTS

Are there any formal volunteering organizations for us techies?

Of course: Check out **geekcorps.org**, a worldwide organization that sends technical volunteers overseas for one to four months to help small businesses in emerging nations. For an inside peek at one of their projects in Ghana, visit **www.geekhalla.org**. Or, if you live in the New York area, check out **voluntech.org**; they match techies with local nonprofits to help them operate at peak effectiveness. Typical projects include database consulting, Web design, and PC education. California tech volunteers can get plugged in through **compuMentor.org**, a nonprofit that helps community-based organizations and schools. Recent project examples include training public school teachers to use hardware, software, and the Internet; giving PC-purchasing advice to an environmental group; coaching employees through a software upgrade; and networking computers at an after-school center.

What is virtual volunteering?

Virtual volunteering allows busy, disabled, or homebound volunteers to give their time from their own house (or anywhere that a notebook computer will take them). One group, the Chamber (**www.chamber4us.org**), uses virtual volunteers to provide technical support to people with disabilities.

administrative work

You're all in this together

If a charitable organization has an office, then it probably needs volunteer office help—both experienced and inexperienced. Even if you've never worked in an office, you should have no trouble getting a volunteer stint to answer phones, file, photocopy, or stuff envelopes. Most nonprofits rely on volunteers to step forward and help with these crucial tasks.

If you know the organization you'd like to help, simply call and ask for the volunteer coordinator. If they don't have a volunteer coordinator, whoever answers the phones will probably be able to tell you who to talk to. (In many cases, it will be the receptionist.) If you don't know who you'd like to work for, contact

your nearest volunteer center, **www.volunteermatch.org**, or City Cares. They'll work with you to find out where you'll fit, based on your interests and skills.

Administrative work is usually an enjoyable way to bond with other volunteers and staff.

ASK THE EXPERTS

I want to help the chronically ill, but the thought of working with them in a hospice makes me a little nervous. Is there some other way to pitch in?

Office work is a great way to serve a cause you're concerned about when you don't have the necessary time, skills, or nerve for working with patients. Like most nonprofits, your local hospice probably needs routine office help with everything from answering phones to filing to data entry. If you're not ready for a front-line commitment, see if they need help with one-time projects. Most fund-raising efforts require one-time mailings, and it's usually volunteers who make these possible.

What if it's the staff members who don't seem to be acting professionally?

Nonprofit staff members are usually extremely grateful for volunteers and therefore act professionally and treat them with respect. But what if you find yourself volunteering for someone who always shows up late for meetings, cancels projects without letting you know, or has the personality of a drill sergeant? Just because you're not getting paid doesn't mean you shouldn't be respected, so handle these situations as you would in a paying job, with good communication. First, try sitting down with the supervisor to discuss the issue and how it affects you. If you're not getting anywhere, consider having a frank discussion with the supervisor's superior. Nonprofits don't want to lose valuable volunteers, so most will be glad you spoke up.

finance and accounting

Keeping an eye on the bottom line

If you have any experience in finance or accounting, are interested in learning about these areas, or are simply good at arithmetic, most nonprofits can use your help.

Whether it's acting as treasurer for your condominium board, tracking income and expenses for a grassroots organization, or sitting on your church's finance committee, finance and accounting positions are often the most overlooked, underappreciated, and challenging positions available for volunteers.

If you're good with business and numbers—and are willing to be diplomatic—you can often make a valuable contribution. Besides tracking income and expenses and working with budgets, charities often need help with decisions that will have a significant financial

impact on the organization—for example, which space to lease, whether to buy or lease a new van, how to deal with insurance issues. In addition, every organization's board of directors needs a treasurer.

Organizations that have to fill these positions with volunteers are very appreciative of the help and are patient with people who are brave enough to step up to the plate. While you need to be serious and committed about taking on this kind of work, you do *not* have to be a financial expert.

ASK THE EXPERTS

I've volunteered to oversee the finances of a local charity, and it seems as though it should be spending much more frugally. How should I approach this?

Gently. You have been brought on to lend your expertise, so the organization should be open to your suggestions. That being said, it is sometimes difficult for people to change their ways, so make suggestions slowly, explain your perspective, be compassionate about how difficult it is to change, and don't expect things to be different overnight.

I have a talent for preparing income tax returns. Is there any way I can help other people with their returns?

Sure! Volunteer Income Tax Assistance (VITA) programs all over the country allow tax preparers to help low-income taxpayers, members of the armed services, and the elderly with their income taxes. You don't need to be a CPA to help out, and training is provided. Contact your state's CPA society or Accountants for the Public Interest at 410-837-6533 for information about your local program.

boards of directors

Does "Board of Directors" conjure up an image of stuffed shirts sitting around a mahogany conference table in big leather chairs, smoking cigars? Most nonprofit organizations have a board of directors whose job is to make sure the organization keeps moving toward its vision—and you might be surprised how very diverse this important group of people is.

What is a "board," anyway? It's a group of people who have been selected (or recruited, in the case of many nonprofits) to donate their time to help an organization establish its overall business vision—and then help it implement the details.

While some board memberships are by invitation only, smaller organizations welcome board members whose background, passion, and skills fit with their needs. In fact, some grassroots organizations don't have any paid staff members—it's the volunteer board of directors that runs every aspect of the nonprofit's work, including fundraising, developing new programs, and implementing the current ones.

More About Boards

To find out more about the issues that nonprofit board members face, check out current and past issues of Board Café at **www.boardcafe.org**; see the list of Frequently Asked Questions from Board Source at **www.boardsource.org**; or try **nonprofit.about.com/cs/helpforboards/index.htm**.

ASK THE EXPERTS

What exactly does a board member do?

While it varies from board to board, attending monthly board meetings is a common requirement. Generally meeting on the same day every month (say, the third Thursday evening), the directors usually discuss old business, bring up new issues and ideas, and discuss the organization's finances (which are tracked by a volunteer treasurer or the paid bookkeeper). Besides regular meeting attendance, most board members work on committees that have specific functions; network in the community on the board's behalf; and recruit friends and family members to help out with events—and to give donations. In a real sense, the board of directors *is* the organization.

I've been asked to sit on a board, but some of my fellow members don't seem to have the same level of professional business experience I do. Should I be worried?

Because of the complex nature of business, the best boards are composed of a wide variety of people who are invited to join because they have some asset or skill to share. For example, a community-based welfare-to-work organization might have a board that includes a visionary executive with connections to many potential employers; a teacher who understands how disadvantaged adults learn best; a social worker; a former welfare-to-work single mom who has experienced the system and is now gainfully employed; as well as other concerned citizens with connections or skills that can help guide the agency.

now what do I do?

Answers to common questions

What are other ways I can help with fund-raising if I've never done it before?

There are plenty! For a small theater company, sell ad space in the program to local businesses; sell season tickets to the opera via telephone; get bagels and bottled water donated for your favorite charity's fun run; find corporate sponsors for a silent auction or the golf outing; work with the communications team on direct mail solicitations or grant writing; raise money for your son's high school football team; join the capital campaign to raise money for your church or synagogue's new building. Does this sound like hard work? It is, since there's so much competition for a limited amount of funds. But don't worry. In many cases you won't need to reinvent the wheel; you'll be working on teams with seasoned fund-raisers who can show you the ropes. For more on fund-raising see pages 36–37.

I don't know much about event planning, so can I help with just part of the process?

Sure. For smaller organizations, many times you'll be able to chip in resources that you didn't even know you had. For example, maybe your best friend owns a restaurant, so you can offer to get food donations for the holiday party. If you're good with numbers, you can offer to keep track of the event's budget, especially if it seems as if no one knows how much is being spent. Or you can offer to bring fresh flowers from your garden when it becomes clear that the decorations budget was too low.

What are some common administrative needs?

Regardless of the size or type, most nonprofits need administrative help. This includes inputting data collected at an information booth; removing duplicate names from the mailing list; answering telephones while the receptionist is at lunch; or copying and assembling information packets for new-volunteer orientation. Administrative help is vital to any nonprofit's success!

I'm fluent in several languages, but I'm getting rusty because I never use them. Are there any opportunities to use this skill for some good?

Yes. Language banks are volunteer groups that help non-English-speaking people in times of need. Many Red Cross (**www.redcross.org**) chapters, for example, have language banks to ensure that, during times of medical, legal, or other emergencies, non-English-speaking residents have access to a translator or interpreter. Some nonprofit volunteer centers also have emergency language banks for residents who don't speak English, or to help the government agencies and nonprofits that serve this population. Finally, some hospitals have language bank volunteers in order to communicate with patients who have limited English backgrounds.

I'm not a good writer. What are some other ways to help a charity get the word out about its good cause?

Be part of the speaker's bureau that travels to schools, nursing homes, or community events to raise awareness for your cause or organization; hang posters at local businesses; put up flyers on bulletin boards; work with event planners to promote an upcoming event; work with information technology (IT) staff and volunteers to promote a Web site and Internet presence.

Now where do I go?!

CONTACTS

Look Good . . . Feel Better
www.lookgoodfeelbetter.org
Teaches beauty techniques to women with cancer.

Geekcorps
www.geekcorps.org
Sends technical volunteers overseas to help businesses in emerging markets.

Clearinghouse for Volunteer Accounting Services
805-495-6755
www.cvas-usa.org
Matches volunteers with non-profit accounting opportunities.

BOOKS

The Jossey-Bass Guide to Strategic Communications for Nonprofits: A Step-by-Step Guide
By Kathy Bonk, Henry Griggs, and Emily Tynes

Event Planning: The Ultimate Guide to Successful Meetings, Corporate Events, Fundraising Galas, Conferences, Conventions, Incentives and Other Special Events
By Judy Allen

Retire in New York City— Even If You're Not Rich
By Janet Hayes and Rita Henley Jensen
Retiree volunteer opportunities

Gala! The Special Event Planner for Professionals and Volunteers
By Patti Coons

The Business of Special Events: Fund-raising Strategies for Changing Times
By Harry A. Freedman and Karen Feldman

Ten Steps to Fund-raising Success: Choosing the Right Strategy for Your Organization (With CD-ROM)
By Mal Warwick and Stephen Hitchcock

3

Civic involvement

Volunteering locally helps you get to know your neighbors and how your town works.

local involvement

Would you like a single volunteer effort that combines your professional, social, and community lives? Then consider civic volunteering, the backbone of thriving cities and towns. What falls under civic volunteer work? Much indeed: all of those local business volunteer organizations and the various women's and men's groups—not to mention volunteer firefighters and local religious outreach programs.

The key word is *local*. Two of the many advantages to volunteering in your own backyard are getting to know your neighbors and gaining an understanding of how your town works. Other benefits are the networking and socializing you and your family will enjoy. If you're new in town, volunteering for a local civic charity is one of the quickest ways to meet new people.

So where to start? Read on.

ASK THE EXPERTS

Are there opportunities to volunteer through my local chamber of commerce?

Frequently, yes. If you are a professional or small business owner whose main focus is improving your community, you might consider joining your local chamber of commerce. ("Your community" could be either the town where your business is located or the town in which you live.) Most chambers are part of the U.S. Chamber of Commerce (**www.uschamber.org**), and provide members with excellent networking opportunities and a voice in community issues. Whether you are a member or not, volunteer opportunities abound. You can work for the chamber itself (stuffing envelopes or doing other administrative work), flip pancakes for kids at Breakfast with Santa, or serve beer at the Rock Around the Block fund-raiser.

What are the Jaycees?

While chambers of commerce are open to all, the Jaycees (officially called the United States Junior Chamber) are geared toward a younger crowd (21 to 39 years old). The Jaycees are made up of business and professional people whose goal is to improve the community and improve themselves in the process. However, in many communities, Jaycees enlist volunteers to help with particular projects. For instance, a local club might plan and sponsor a haunted house to raise money to buy clothes for the homeless; link up with local schools to provide tutoring for kids; or participate in Christmas in April to rehabilitate a needy family's home. For more information, call 800-529-2337 or click to **www.usjaycees.org**.

business and professional organizations

Service and socializing

A number of nonprofit organizations bring together local professionals and businesspeople to better their communities, their businesses, and themselves. These clubs focus on community service, friendship, and promoting high ethical standards; they also provide excellent networking opportunities. In fact, many small business owners and professionals consider their volunteer efforts in these clubs to be critical to their professional success. The most established groups are listed below.

Rotary The club's motto is "service above self." Rotarians serve their community both locally and internationally. After members have been involved locally, they are drawn to volunteer internationally (see pages 174–193 for opportunities abroad). For more information, go to **www.rotary.org** or check your local white pages.

Lions The Lions Clubs have 1.4 million members in 187 countries, and put their emphasis on blindness prevention and assistance. Clubs often raise money for Seeing-Eye dog schools and solicit donations of refurbished eyeglasses, which are given to the visually impaired. Get in touch with Lions Clubs at 630-571-5466 or **www.lionsclubs.org**.

Kiwanis With more than 600,000 members in 76 countries, this club's primary emphasis is on social networking and community service. In some towns, the fourth Friday of September is Peanut Day, when club members solicit at grocery stores and corner stop signs to raise money. Call Kiwanis International at 317-875-8755 or click to **www.kiwanis.org**.

Members in these groups pay dues—usually less than $100 a year. Besides the usual volunteering benefits, membership generally earns group discounts on hotels and rental cars, auto club membership, and even insurance.

ⒶSK THE EXPERTS

What kinds of volunteer work do these groups do?

It depends on what the community needs. Members might raise money for local charitable requests, for instance, with a Rotary car wash to help the local YMCA purchase educational materials for its after-school program. Other groups might focus on local beautification by planting trees in designated parks or adopting vacant lots and converting them into flower gardens.

I'd like to attend a Kiwanis meeting. Do I have to be invited?

No, you don't have to be invited to a Kiwanis meeting. Simply find out when your local chapter meets by calling 317-875-8755. You might want to talk to the director of your chapter first, however, to make sure that your particular club is involved in projects that interest you.

A Kiwanis volunteer reads to elementary school children, underscoring the organization's focus on bringing children and books together.

women's groups

Not just mint juleps

Once upon a time, few development and service opportunities were available for women. So, in true American fashion, women started their own groups.

One of the oldest women's groups is the Junior League. The Association of Junior Leagues International (**www.ajli.org**) provides volunteering opportunities to women who seek to improve their communities. Women who join and become actively involved often get a wide range of training and education in management, facilitating, public speaking, and other areas.

To date, there are approximately 300 Junior Leagues worldwide. Each league canvasses locally to determine the community's needs. While volunteer programs vary widely, most focus on children and family programs, women's health education, and the improvement of local parks and playgrounds. Junior League annual dues range anywhere from $75 to $400, depending on the chapter. And in most leagues, you have to be sponsored by a member to join.

Another women's organization is the American Association of University Women (AAUW). Its goal is "promoting education and equity for all women and girls," with an emphasis on education and legal advocacy. There are 1,500 branches nationwide. Membership (with various dues levels) is open to college students and graduates. Contact **www.aauw.org** or 800-326-2289.

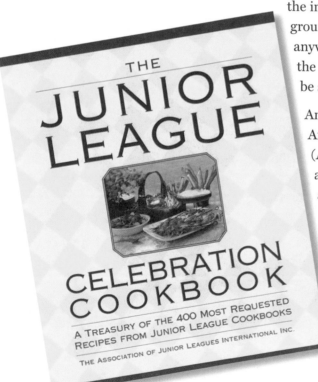

THE
JUNIOR
LEAGUE

CELEBRATION
COOKBOOK
A TREASURY OF THE 400 MOST REQUESTED
RECIPES FROM JUNIOR LEAGUE COOKBOOKS
THE ASSOCIATION OF JUNIOR LEAGUES INTERNATIONAL INC.

One of the more popular fund-raising efforts is a local cookbook, with recipes from members.

ASK THE EXPERTS

I owe a lot of my career success to older women who helped me along. Where do I go to give back by mentoring younger professional women?

The National Association of Female Executives at 800-634-6233 or **www.nafe.com**, is a professional organization that helps women meet their business and career goals. Its 200 chapters, which are all run by volunteers, need women leaders to mentor other women, to serve on the local boards of directors, to create the local newsletter, and to search out speakers for monthly events. Your local Junior League and YWCA may also have mentoring opportunities.

Are there other options besides the usual women's groups?

Yes: Contact your local YWCA. This organization focuses on a wide range of needs for both women and girls, and in different stages of their lives. The more than 300 YWCA's in the U.S. vary widely in size, resources, and programs. Some have childcare centers that need volunteers to baby-sit while staff are being trained. Others maintain women's shelters and need volunteers to help out. Finally, YWCA's need help with back-office and fund-raising tasks.

Do I need to hold any specific beliefs to volunteer at the YWCA?

No you don't. While YWCA originally stood for the Young Women's Christian Association, the organization no longer has any religious affiliations.

Any other women's groups?

Altrusa International, at 312-427-4410 or **www.altrusa.com**, focuses on literacy but also helps abused women and others. Zonta International, at 312-930-5848 or **www.zonta.org**, helps women become self-sufficient and provides scholarships.

garden clubs and other hobby groups

More than pretty flowers

While most volunteer groups are organized around the need they serve (for example, Volunteers for Literacy), a lot of volunteer work is the offshoot of membership in hobby clubs. One of the largest hobby clubs in America is the National Garden Clubs.

Since 1891, members have been sharing their love of plants and flowers with like-minded souls—and along the way, doing good works. For example, the Garden Club of New Smyrna Beach, Florida, takes care of the local hospital's flower beds and sponsors a yearly fund-raiser for the local high school students' art league.

Like many volunteer organizations, Garden Clubs has a national headquarters that helps start new clubs and provides members with educational materials and gardening study courses. It also sponsors national events, including National Garden Week. Dues usually are no more than $20 or $30 a year.

To find the garden club nearest you, visit **www.gardenclub.org** or call 314-776-7574.

Proceeds from garden club flower shows often go to city landscaping or beautification of streets or highways.

ASK THE EXPERTS

I love to cook, but I'm not very interested in traditional cooking clubs. Any ideas on how cooks can make a contribution?

Many people start hobby clubs, with members drawn from their workplace or neighborhood. The idea is to bring together people who have something in common—in your case, a love of cooking. Members can then contribute to the common good by donating some (or even all) the dishes they make to the local soup kitchen or food drive.

I'm enthusiastic about collecting baseball cards. How can I turn this hobby into a volunteer opportunity?

Why not take the initiative and start your own collector's club? Once you've rounded up a group of like-minded souls, you can brainstorm and come up with volunteering ideas. Perhaps you could show your baseball cards to a Boys & Girls Club one afternoon and introduce the children to the art of collecting.

TURNING POINT

I was thrilled when I was elected president of my local garden club. I also had great ideas for our local fund-raiser. But while most of the women were wonderful, one was very disrespectful. In fact, her critical remarks about her committee caused a number of new members to leave. Although I didn't know how to handle her, I knew I had to so something for the good of the club. So I decided to ask her to lunch so we could talk about our work. Over dessert, I finally got my courage up, and I told her I had noticed how sharp she had been with some new members. I then gently asked if anything was troubling her. It turns out she was going through a bitter divorce and was experiencing some health problems as well. When I suggested that she take a leave of absence from her garden club duties, she was obviously relieved. A lesson learned: Volunteers have lives too, and sometimes they need help as much as anybody else.

—Karen N., Nashville, Tennessee

fire fighting

Everyday heroes

According to the National Volunteer Fire Council, nearly 80% of this country's firefighters are not paid for their services, as important as they are. Small towns rely the most on volunteers, who usually make up 100% of the force. Midsize towns often use a combination of paid and unpaid firefighters.

In most cases, the tab for training and equipment (it can run into the thousands of dollars) will be picked up by the department, which is often funded with county, state, and federal money, as well as by private donations. Because of the big tab, trainees are asked to make a commitment before training begins. While not specifically designed to weed people out, training programs sometimes have that effect. New recruits must pass extremely challenging physical tests before being allowed to serve. For more information, click to the National Volunteer Fire Council Web site at **www.nvfc.org**.

Once you're on the job, you'll not only be on the monthly on-call schedule (where you are required to respond to alarms), you'll have "drill nights" (usually once a month), be required to take refresher courses, and contribute time to fund-raisers.

Because volunteer firefighters are needed so desperately, some areas offer retirement benefits to encourage people to join. If you're interested in becoming a firefighter, consult your local fire department or call 800-347-3546 to learn about opportunities in your community.

A volunteer group that often works side by side with firefighters is the emergency medical technicians—volunteers who respond to ambulance calls. You don't have to be a doctor or nurse to be an EMT, but you do have to go through rigorous training.

ASK THE EXPERTS

What sort of training is required to be a firefighter?

A lot. To begin with, all firefighters—paid or unpaid—must undergo 150 hours of intense training. Certain departments may require more training for specialized tasks, such as emergency medical service, hazardous materials, terrorism, or search and rescue.

I'm not ready to get involved directly with the fire department. Is there any other way I could help?

Yes. Consider joining the International Fire Buff Associates (**www.ifba.org**). It has over 80 independent organizations whose members support their local department. These self-proclaimed "fire geeks" stage fund-raising events, help restore antique fire engines, and share fire-related memorabilia. Contact the IFBA or your local firehouse to see if there's a chapter near you.

Can women become volunteer firefighters?

Absolutely! Women in Fire Service (**www.wfsi.org**) estimates that as many as 30,000 to 40,000 of the country's volunteer fire-fighters are women.

religious groups

Doing God's work

If you faithfully attend your local house of worship, you probably already know whether the staff needs volunteer help. But even if you're an infrequent churchgoer, don't overlook opportunities that have to do with religion.

Many religious groups work hard to reach out to the community. Some houses of worship have partnerships with local homeless shelters, nursing homes, and mentoring and tutoring programs. By volunteering through your church, temple, or mosque rather than approaching the volunteer organizations directly, you can enhance your experience by serving alongside people who have similar values and interests.

Most houses of worship also need volunteers to help with their own administrative and fund-raising duties, work on the newsletter, organize and teach religion classes for children, help the elderly and people with special needs, and welcome new members. On holidays, they might need help conducting services and keeping everything running smoothly.

ASK THE EXPERTS

The only time I attend services is during the holidays. This year I want to get more involved. What can I do?

During special holiday seasons, your congregation's paid staff is usually overloaded and needs both administrative and liturgical help. For Christians, the busy seasons are Advent (just before Christmas) and Holy Week (just before Easter). For Jews, the busy seasons are in the fall—leading up to the High Holy Days (Rosh Hashana and Yom Kippur) and during festivals like Passover, Purim, and Chanukah. Often, any decorating and hospitality committees need extra help during these seasons.

My only free days are on the weekend. Will I still be able to help?

It often takes dozens of volunteers just to pull off a weekly service. Most churches and synagogues, for example, need greeters to welcome their parishioners, ushers to seat latecomers, and people to drive congregants to and from the service. Most of the musicians and singers each week are volunteers, and new talent is always welcomed. Rehearsals are often required, however, so don't think you'll be able to just show up on Sunday morning and belt out a hymn.

military organizations

Show your thanks to the men and women in uniform

American citizens are entitled to armed services protection, but there are many ways to support—and say thank you—to the men and women who protect our country. Although most volunteer opportunities are geared to military retirees or families, there are also a few for civilians. (Keep in mind that for security reasons, access to military bases—especially during times of heightened security—is often restricted.)

The organization that primarily recruits civilians to serve U.S. Army soldiers is the Army Community Service, which has a wide variety of volunteering opportunities. Among them are teaching money-management classes, preparing income taxes, and preparing foreign-born soldiers for citizenship. To get in touch with the Army Community Service, contact your nearest military installation and ask for the volunteer coordinator. For more information, visit **www.goacs.org**.

The retired historic lightship Relief, a floating lighthouse for years, served as the cover of the annual report of the Navy-Marine Corps Relief Society, a nonprofit organization that gives financial, educational, and other help to Navy personnel and their families.

To offer help to the Navy or Marines, you can join the Navy-Marine Corps Relief Society (NMCRS), a nonprofit organization providing emergency financial relief to members of the Navy and the Marines. Operating in over 200 offices (both on land and afloat) throughout the world, the NMCRS provides emergency financial, educational, and other help to Navy and Marine personnel and their families. Volunteer opportunities include teaching Budget for Baby workshops (for expectant or new parents) and working at one of the many thrift shops that sell low-cost clothes and household goods to people in the services. To find the NMCRS nearest you, visit their Web site (**www.nmcrs.org**) or check the white pages of your phone book.

ASK THE EXPERTS

Are there any short-term opportunities to see if working with these groups is suitable for me?

Often thousands of miles from home, sailors and soldiers find being welcomed by local families to be a big morale booster. Some bases have official Adopt-A-Sailor/Adopt-A-Soldier programs during the holidays, when you can open your home to soldiers to share a meal. But you don't have to wait for the holidays to extend yourself. You can call at any time simply to invite a lonely serviceman or servicewoman to attend a local museum, the St. Patrick's Day parade, or a hot-air balloon festival—anything to make soldiers or sailors feel welcome in the town where they're stationed. Contact your nearest naval base and check with its public affairs department or its senior enlisted advisor; they will let you know if their base has such a program and how to get involved.

I'm a civilian nurse, but I'm very interested in helping the military. Is there anything I can do?

Yes. Contact the Navy-Marine Corps Relief Society and find out about their Visiting Nurse program. This program uses both volunteer and paid nurses to provide servicemen with health education and other information about health-related resources. All military bases have military hospitals that need volunteers—contact their public affairs office. There are even a few military retirement homes that need help.

What is the USO?

During World War I, several nonprofit organizations banded together to create the United Service Organizations (USO). This entity, which isn't directly connected to either the military or the government, serves the men and women of the armed forces by giving them a "home away from home." USOs are usually located at airports, military bases, and large cities, and need volunteers to answer phones, work at the information desk, or tidy up the kitchen and refreshment center. To volunteer, contact your local USO by visiting their Web site at **www.uso.org**, calling 202-610-5700, or checking your local white pages.

now what do I do?
Answers to common questions

Do fraternal organizations provide members with community service opportunities?

In some cases, yes. Just remember that "fraternal" means that the focus might be more social than service oriented. That said, find out what your local groups are up to. These groups, like Moose International (**www.mooseintl.org**) or the Elks (**www.elks.org**), might support local nonprofit organizations such as homeless shelters, food pantries, Adopt-A-Highway programs, Boy Scout troops, Big Brothers organizations, veterans centers, and Meals on Wheels programs. The primary focus of the Shriners (**www.shrinershq.org**) is fund-raising for its 22 children's hospitals.

I'm a stay-at-home mom. Can I join the Chamber of Commerce or one of the service clubs—say, Kiwanis or Lions?

Usually, yes. Since the focus of these groups is often service, where you work doesn't really matter. Chambers of commerce often have separate membership levels for residents in the area, and Kiwanis and Lions clubs welcome nonprofessionals. Attend a meeting as a guest to check out what the chamber or club has to offer, to help you decide.

How can I get involved in teaching safety classes?

If you like teaching and are interested in safety, then the Red Cross offers a number of opportunities. You can be trained to teach their Basic Aid Training class (which covers what to do in an emergency) and babysitter certification classes. Training is also necessary before teaching CPR, first aid, and water safety. Once you're a teacher, you can set your own hours with your local chapter, depending on your skills and availability.

I don't have enough free time to join a volunteering organization, but I would still like to help. What can I do?

Self-starters can choose from any number of one-time volunteer jobs. Consider organizing a one-day neighborhood cleanup. Or volunteer to help out one morning in your local school. If you have a hobby or special skill, offer to talk about it at your library. The goal is to share your time with others and make a difference. And the sky's the limit!

Does the Coast Guard need volunteers?

The U.S. Coast Guard Auxiliary helps the Coast Guard promote boating safety. Nearly 33,000 volunteers receive special training so that they can help the Coast Guard with public education, boating safety checks and patrols, search and rescue, and marine environmental protection. The CGA is active in over 2,000 U.S. cities and annually saves almost 500 lives, helps 15,000 distressed boaters, conducts over 150,000 free boating-safety checks, and teaches students about boating and water safety. Contact the CGA at 877-875-6296 or **www.cgaux.org**.

Now where do I go?!

CONTACTS

Catholic Charities
703-549-1390
www.catholiccharitiesusa.org
Over 1,400 local agencies and institutions geared toward community service.

USAFreedomCorps
www.USAFreedomCorps.gov
Comprehensive clearinghouse for finding local volunteering opportunities.

Clubs that combine local volunteering with networking and friendship:

Rotary International
www.rotary.org

Lions Clubs
630-571-5466
www.lionsclubs.org

Kiwanis
317-875-8755
www.kiwanis.org

National Garden Clubs
314-776-7574
www.gardenclub.org

National Volunteer Fire Council
800-347-3546
www.nvfc.org

United Services Organization
202-610-5700
www.uso.org
Serving the men and women who serve our country.

BOOKS

100 Ways to Strengthen & Unify Our Country
By Jennifer Lee

Visions of Charity: Volunteer Workers and Moral Community
By Rebecca Anne Allahyari

Thoughts on Fire: Life Lessons of a Volunteer Firefighter
By Frank B. McCluskey

Service Clubs in American Society: Rotary, Kiwanis, and Lions
By Jeffrey A. Charles

Putting Faith in Neighborhoods: Making Cities Work through Grassroots Citizenship
By Stephen Goldsmith and Ryan Streeter (Contributor)

4

Social action

Without the involvement of concerned citizens, changes in our social fabric could never occur.

the political process

People power

Participating in the political and electoral process is the responsibility of every American citizen. It is also a privilege in which volunteers play an essential role. What exactly do volunteers do to help implement social action? Their efforts cover everything from getting out the vote to shaping social policy.

Volunteers are also needed to help shape social thought. Without the involvement of concerned citizens, changes in our social fabric could never occur. Direct citizen action has helped pass countless laws, including many we now take for granted, such as those regulating seat-belt use and limiting pollution.

When it comes to informing the public, volunteers are vital. They do everything from getting the word out to registering people to vote. Volunteering is also not too complicated, since you really don't need any special skills or knowledge to help. To get involved, you only need to work with a local group that is actively involved in the process, such as a political party, a community board, or a local advocacy group.

ASK THE EXPERTS

What is the League of Women Voters?

The League of Women Voters is a nonpartisan organization whose members work to improve voting and political processes through education and advocacy. Each local league operates differently, but all provide a variety of services to local voters. Local chapters host forums and invite candidates to discuss the issues; they work preelection hot lines to answer voter questions about the issues or to provide directions to the polling place; and they study local issues and develop informational booklets that help citizens to understand the issues. While many volunteer opportunities are available, most chapters require membership. Contact them at **www.lwv.org** or check the white pages for your local chapter. And no, you do not have to be a woman to join the League of Women Voters. Since the 1970s, it has been open to men, who make up approximately 10% of its current membership.

Do you need to know a lot about politics and the voting process to join the League of Women Voters?

No! Anyone who is interested in learning more about community issues or how your local government works is welcome. No previous knowledge or experience is necessary.

election volunteers

Making democracy work,
one vote at a time

Ever wonder how elections actually happen? There is so much to do: prepare the voting space, get the voting machines in place, check each voter's registration and vote history—the work is endless. And for the most part it's done by volunteers.

One of the key volunteers in elections is the **election judge**—an ordinary citizen who is a "judge" in name only. Judges work from dawn until dusk on election day, ensuring that the voting process runs smoothly. While technically not a volunteer position (judges get paid for the day at the polls, and sometimes for their training), it is generally done as a labor of love and sign of appreciation for the civic process.

Elections, whether for president of the United States or the passage of a local bond issue, need several election judges. What do they do? Judges are expected to arrive at a polling place an hour before voting begins. They open the doors; set up tables, booths, and other voting equipment; greet and register voters and provide them with ballots; and record and certify totals.

League of Women Voters volunteers also assist in the process by being available to help out on that very busy day. For example, they might deliver supplies to a polling place that needs more pencils or has run out of ballots.

One thing to keep in mind: Communities use a combination of Republican and Democratic judges, so be prepared to state your party affiliation. Some states require an even number of Republicans and Democrats at each polling place; others require the district's majority party to provide more judges.

ASK THE EXPERTS

What sort of training is required to be an election judge? Is it more than a one-day commitment?

Election judge training is usually a simple session for a few hours. While there, you learn about the printed forms, voting procedures, what to watch for during the voting process, and how to tally votes.

How can I become an election judge?

Call or write your local county clerk or election commission for information. Sometimes voter registration cards have a section to complete if you're interested in becoming an election judge.

party politics

Elephants, donkeys, and other political animals

While the two major parties in the United States are the Democratic and the Republican, there are many others. The Reform Party, the Green Party, and the Libertarian Party—to name just a few—have all gained followers in recent years. Be they large or small, political parties depend on lots of local volunteers, and there are plenty of ways to get involved.

Maybe you feel strongly about a particular candidate. If so, contact her office and ask how you can help. Most local offices need administrative help with tasks like mailings, answering phones, and passing out literature. They often have a volunteer coordinator who can help you decide where to pitch in.

More likely, you simply want to help a particular political party. In order to avoid divisiveness, the parties themselves are most active after the primaries, when there's only one party candidate running for each office. You can volunteer for your local chapter of the Republican National Committee, Democratic National Committee, or another political party.

TURNING POINT

Since I lost my job right around election time, I decided to spend some of my free time volunteering in the local headquarters for the Republican Party. I started out just answering the phones, but the office was so short-staffed in other areas that I ended up handing out flyers at bus stops and train stations, asking people to put signs on their lawns, and actively seeking other ways to help out. When the office manager quit unexpectedly, they asked me to take over. Not only did I accept, but I love my new job!

—Bryan P., Dallas, Texas

ASK THE EXPERTS

What's a precinct?

It's a subdivision of a voting ward. Parties break up their state
and city organizations into precincts so they can respond better to
the needs of each individual constituency. Depending on your
county and state, you might have the opportunity to be a precinct
committeeman or a precinct captain. These volunteer positions,
which are sometimes elected and sometimes appointed, represent
your local precinct. These jobs call for circulating petitions to
nominate candidates, helping the party's voter turnout, and
appointing election judges. These are good positions for people
who enjoy talking with and meeting people, and who feel strongly
about their party.

community boards

Making decisions for the
good of the group

Elected officials aren't the only ones who have a voice in government affairs. On the local level, there are community service boards (or commissions). These boards, composed of volunteers, provide advisory services to their local governments. For example, most towns have a zoning board whose job is to review plans for new buildings or new businesses to make sure they fit in with the local zoning laws. (Most towns also have a board of education. For more on that see pages 126–127.)

Most towns also have boards to oversee their town parks and any cultural efforts. For example, the arts commission in Redmond, Washington, is concerned with the performing arts and arts education issues. Arts commission members hold separate monthly meetings to initiate projects. One project, Art Outside the Box, brought in local children to paint artwork on utility boxes around town. One subcommittee worked with local stores to donate paint and other supplies; another worked to find and supervise the kids who did the artwork.

How do you get on a community board? In some towns, the mayor appoints the board; in others, the communities accumulate applications for positions, should an opening arise. If you are interested in a particular board and your city or village doesn't accept advance applications, call the mayor's office and ask how you can find out when an opening becomes available.

**Citizens in one city painted municipal
trash cans, turning them into public art.**

ASK THE EXPERTS

What are some typical boards?

They vary from place to place, but some are fairly
common. Civil service boards oversee issues related to
the police and fire department. Design review boards
look at building applications to determine if the proposed work is compatible with the city. Library boards
oversee the library's policy and how its events and
services are publicized. Trails commissions recommend
action about hiking, biking, horse, water, and pedestrian
trails. Zoning review boards make recommendations
to the city about zoning and conditional-use permits.
Finally, beautification boards oversee decisions affect-
ing local beautification.

How big a commitment is it to become a board member?

It's a big commitment. Board members serve for a particular
term—anywhere from two years to six years—and are often reappoint-
ed. Once appointed to a board, members attend regular meetings—
anywhere from one to four times a month—and may need to perform
other tasks during the month, such as conducting research for the
board or sitting on one of the board's subcommittees.

watchdog groups

Self-appointed protectors

While elected officials, city councils, and community boards make the actual decisions that impact a community, local constituents and watchdog organizations can influence how these decisions get made.

Most watchdog organizations started with one person, passionate to make local changes. For example, Mothers Against Drunk Driving was started in 1980 by a mother whose daughter was killed by a repeat DWI offender. MADD eventually influenced state and local legislatures to strengthen drunk driving laws. Another example of a watchdog group is the Parents Television Council (**www.parentstv.org**), a group that monitors TV content.

Watchdog groups also monitor the news and newspapers, and contact journalists and publishers if their reports are distorted or inaccurate. And they keep an eye on how the government spends money and how politicians vote.

If there is a cause that you want to look out for, see if a national organization has a local chapter in your neighborhood (check the Internet or your telephone book). If there is a national organization but no local chapter, consider opening one. While it might sound like a big responsibility, you would receive guidance and support from the national office.

Parents Television Council

Join or form a grassroots chapter of the Parents Television Council, which uses this rating system to indicate what programs are appropriate for family viewing.

Green Light
Family-friendly show promoting responsible themes and traditional values.

Yellow Light
The show contains adult-oriented themes and dialogue that may be inappropriate for youngsters.

Red Light
Show may include gratuitous sex, explicit dialogue, violent content, or obscene language, and is unsuitable for children.

ASK THE EXPERTS

What do watchdog groups do, and what do they need help with?

Watchdog groups are usually grassroots organizations, originally started by a few people who felt that a large group entrusted with the public good was dropping the ball. The object of many watches is the government, specifically lawmakers. Other targets include utility companies or the media. In addition to the skills listed in Chapter 2, watchdog groups need help getting people involved and lobbying lawmakers (with phone calls, letter-writing campaigns and face-to-face meetings).

Do watchdog groups really make a difference?

Yes! These groups can raise public awareness about an issue, which often causes the public officials in charge to be more attentive. Police departments and district attorneys, for example, are often more vigilant in the neighborhoods where there is a local MADD chapter.

community policing

Many local communities participate in Neighborhood Watch (or Block Watch, Town Watch, Crime Watch), which is associated with the National Crime Prevention Council (**www.ncpc.org** or 202-466-6272).

These Watch groups are essentially serving as volunteer eyes and ears for the local police. By forging bonds among neighbors and establishing relationships with the police, they often resolve burglaries and robberies.

In Chicago, for example, the Chicago Alternative Policing Strategy unites the police and the community to identify and solve neighborhood crime issues, like abandoned buildings and cars, vacant lots, drug houses, and graffiti. By attending monthly meetings, providing input, and getting to know local "beat" officers, residents help keep their communities safe.

If your community is part of a Neighborhood Watch, consider joining. If your community does not participate in Neighborhood Watch, you might form one in your neighborhood.

STEP BY STEP

Organizing a Neighborhood Watch

Organizing a Neighborhood Watch is a low-cost way to reduce (or prevent) crime in your neighborhood, as well as make your community a safer and friendlier place to live. Participating neighbors look out for one another's property; notify the policy of any suspicious neighborhood activity; and work to make their communities a better place. (See **www.ncpc.org** for more details.)

1. Form a small planning committee with your neighbors to discuss the Watch concept, local issues, and possible obstacles.

2. Plan an initial neighborhood meeting to see how interested your other neighbors might be.

3. Contact your local police department to discuss neighborhood crime issues and invite a representative to the initial meeting.

4. Publicize the meeting by distributing flyers door-to-door and making follow-up phone calls.

5. At the initial meeting, explain the Watch concept, discuss neighborhood concerns and issues, and decide whether or not to adopt a Watch program.

6. If your neighbors agree to adopt the program, a volunteer chairperson should be elected to oversee the program. Be aware that there is good chance the person elected will be you, since organizations often select the originator of the idea to run the program.

7. Each block should have a block captain to communicate with neighbors and act as a liaison with the police and the chairperson.

8. Another volunteer should prepare a neighborhood map that includes names, addresses, phone numbers, and e-mail addresses of participants.

now what do I do?
Answers to common questions

What is a referendum?

A referendum is a proposed law that citizens vote on directly during the election process. If there is an issue that you would like to see your community vote on, consider working to get a referendum on the ballot. There are two ways to do this. Certain units of government (like schools, libraries, and fire departments) can add a referendum to the ballot. This means attending meetings, and getting your voice heard is key. The other route is to circulate a petition. If you secure a certain number of signatures, your issue will be included on the ballot. With either route, by banding together with like-minded friends and neighbors, your action can result in concrete changes to your community.

Is there any real difference between volunteering for a party and volunteering for a candidate?

While many of the functions may be the same (distributing literature, hosting events, making get-out-the-vote calls), volunteers for the party are more likely to undertake the larger organizational tasks, especially that of registering voters. Also, candidates within the same party may run against one another in a primary, so much hard work needs to be done before the general election even starts.

I'd like to help my local boards, but I can't make that kind of commitment. Are there any periodic opportunities for me?

Often these boards can use your help—even if you are not an official board member. You might help them plan and organize events that they run. For example, Redmond, Washington's arts council has an annual literary event called Write Out Loud that sponsors writing contests and poetry slams. Volunteers help plan this event, put up signs, register participants, set up chairs, and perform other one-time tasks.

I'm on the road for my job a lot, but I often have extra time on the airplane or in my hotel room. How can I pitch in from my laptop?

Virtual volunteering is becoming more and more common, especially among the disabled, information technology professionals, and traveling professionals like yourself. Some watchdog organizations use volunteers to track court cases in order to see how issue-related cases are being decided. To find out more, contact your local watchdog group, or check out the virtual volunteering opportunities at **www.volunteermatch.org**.

Now where do I go?!

CONTACTS

Volunteer Match
www.volunteermatch.org
Internet clearinghouse for volunteer positions.

Idealist
www.idealist.org/
Also known as Action Without Borders, it's a global network of more than 29,000 groups in 153 countries working to build a world where all people can live free and dignified lives.

National Crime Prevention Council
202-466-6272
www.ncpc.org

Volunteers in Police Service
www.policevolunteers.org
Part of the newly created Citizen Corps, Volunteers in Police Service lets citizens help their local police force.

BOOKS

Soul of a Citizen: Living With Conviction in a Cynical Time
By Paul Rogat Loeb

The Democracy Owners' Manual: A Practical Guide to Changing the World
By Jim Shultz

The State We're In: Washington
By the League of Women Voters of Washington Education Fund

5

Neighbors in need

One interesting benefit to volunteering is that you get to meet people who need your help.

helping the needy

What images come to mind when you think about people you could help by volunteering? Most likely, they are of the homeless and the hungry, abused women and children, and other unfortunates caught in bad circumstances.

Caring for those in need is central to nearly every religious or moral code. Call it charity, the Golden Rule, or whatever you like—we are needed to tend to people in difficult circumstances, just as we would hope they would do for us if roles were reversed.

A Lions Club volunteer passes out treats in Venezuela after a flood.

Sometimes this means assisting people with a tangible need, like feeding the hungry or finding temporary housing for a family whose home was destroyed in a fire. Sometimes it means helping address the underlying issues: Education and awareness programs can help prevent everything from domestic violence to drug abuse to repeat offenses by ex-convicts. And sometimes it simply means being a friend to a lonely elderly man or woman or a welfare-to-work mom.

ASK THE EXPERTS

Can I really make a difference by volunteering?

Can you, by yourself, solve world hunger or eliminate homelessness? No, and don't expect to. But can you help feed a single person (or even several!) and help a mentally ill individual or runaway teenager find a bed for the night? Absolutely.

Why should I help, when many of these homeless or jailed folks are just suffering the consequences of their own choices?

It's not always that simple. The family that we are born into (and the resulting education, resources, and guidance) has a great impact on our choices. Most incarcerated people, for example, often lack basic education and life skills that could help them make the right decisions in the future. Many suffer from mental illness. And many women find themselves homeless as the result of domestic violence.

One interesting benefit to volunteering with the disadvantaged is that you get to meet people firsthand who need your help. After getting to know them, you may alter your preconceived ideas about the homeless or prisoners.

violence against women

Giving them shelter and support

Each year, more than one million women seek medical assistance for injuries caused by abuse. Another five million will be battered but will not seek treatment. Approximately 35% of all women with children in homeless shelters cite domestic violence as the primary cause of their homelessness.

Shelters provide a safe haven for women and their children. They provide room and board and help with medical, transportation, financial, and other immediate needs. Supported through public funds and private donations, these nonprofits generally operate on shoestring budgets and need your help.

Volunteers answer the house phones (or a crisis line, if they have one), work in the house itself (sorting, organizing, and handing out donations received, like clothes and toiletries), and do light housecleaning or maintenance (painting, decorating, and gardening). Depending on your background and skills, you might even be able to sit in on a support group and learn how to facilitate a group of your own.

Other opportunities include providing intake services (helping women when they first arrive at the shelter and determining their needs) and working with the children of abused women.

All of this may sound pretty intense, and it is. But most shelters provide training for their volunteers—as much as 30 to 40 hours—during which they learn about domestic violence, interact with victims and their children, and are shown how that particular shelter operates. In return, there might be a slight charge for the training or an ongoing commitment of your time.

ASK THE EXPERTS

How can I start working at a shelter?

If you feel drawn to volunteering for a shelter, call your local shelter and ask to talk with the volunteer coordinator. For the safety of the residents, the centers are usually not that easy to find. If you can't find a local shelter in the yellow pages (under Domestic Violence or Women's Shelters), look up your state's coalition against domestic violence or contact the National Coalition Against Domestic Violence at 303-839-1852 or **www.ncadv.org**. Because of the sensitive nature of these situations, you should expect screening and background checks before you are allowed to volunteer.

Are there other volunteer needs that women's shelters could use?

Fund-raising and other skills, including clerical, legal, and even massage therapist services are needed at most shelters. In addition, shelters often train their volunteers to raise public awareness by speaking in schools, to women's groups, or anywhere else information on domestic violence is needed.

Helping Victims of Rape

Rape crisis centers, which are sometimes combined with domestic violence shelters, provide immediate resources to sexual assault victims, often meeting them at the hospital or police department and helping with any initial problems that arise. As the survivor continues to recover, these centers give referrals to support groups, therapy, and other psychological resources. They also help victims as they interact with doctors, police, lawyers, and other professionals on the case. The centers also provide education on the issue of sexual violence. Most centers have 24-hour hot lines that give information and referrals and even offer support programs for the victim's loved ones. Most rape crisis centers rely heavily on volunteers. If you are interested in volunteering your services, you can visit **www.hopeforhealing.org/crisiscenters.html** to find the center nearest you, or contact your local YWCA. For most volunteer positions, you'll need to undergo 30 to 50 hours of training before starting.

children in need

Abused, neglected,
in need of help

One of the many special rewards of helping children in need is that your efforts can not only help a child for the present but can help prevent problems as the child grows. There are a number of avenues available to help fulfill these children's needs.

The Child Welfare League of America, an association of more than 1,100 public and private nonprofit agencies that helps over 3.5 million abused and neglected children and families each year, can put you in touch with one of six regional centers throughout the country. The centers can then help you find a volunteering opportunity to match your skills, interests, and geographical location.

The aid agencies need volunteers to help educate teen moms (or teens at risk of pregnancy), spend time with children whose parents are in jail, and provide an alternative to gang membership. In addition, these children often need mentoring and tutoring. Contact the CWLA at 202-638-2952 or **www.cwla.org**.

If you're not sure where to begin, contact your nearest volunteer center or **www.volunteermatch.com** or **www.usafreedomcorps.gov**, United Way, or City Cares. They can help place you in a child-assistance position that suits you best. As with any sensitive volunteering position, expect screenings and background checks before you can serve.

ASK THE EXPERTS

It seems that helping children might require quite a commitment on my part. What are some one-time volunteer opportunities?

One opportunity that doesn't require an extensive commitment is teaching a parenting class. (Contact your local child-abuse prevention agency to see if they run such programs.) Or you can buy gifts for needy families during the holiday season. You might get involved with foster parents who live in your community, offering to lend them a hand with errands or babysitting. Contact the National Foster Parents Association at 800-557-5238 or **www.nfpainc.org**.

I'd like to do more than tutor or mentor children once a week. Are there other ways to help?

Consider becoming a Court Appointed Special Advocate, who is assigned to abuse and neglect cases by a judge. Special advocates research the case, talk with everyone related to it (including the child, parents, and other family members), and objectively report to the court what they believe is best for the child. This helps the judge make decisions about custody and other issues that affect the child. Throughout the court's involvement with the case (which could last up to a year or more), advocates monitor the child's situation and remain a presence as the case moves through the maze of the child welfare system. Visit **www.nationalcasa.org** or call 800-628-3233 to learn of a CASA program near you. CASA's 40-hour training program will provide the necessary in-depth education about the court process, child development, abuse and neglect, and other topics.

senior citizens

Shut in, shut out, and sometimes, just lonely

As our life expectancies increase and the baby boom generation barrels toward old age, the need for volunteers to work with the elderly will only increase.

What can you do to assist? Plenty. You can help older adults keep track of their finances by helping them organize and pay their bills. Or drive them to a doctor's appointment. How to find seniors who could use some help? Contact your local nursing home or assisted-living center and ask for the volunteer coordinator.

Visit a nursing home as a volunteer for Little Brothers/Friends of the Elderly. Here a volunteer gives a facial.

If you're looking for an ongoing commitment (one year minimum), sign up to be a Visiting Volunteer for Little Brothers/Friends of the Elderly (**www.littlebrothers.org** or 312-829-3055). After a brief training and orientation meeting, you'll be paired with an elderly friend. Some volunteers visit seniors who live alone and might enjoy sharing a meal or social activity with other seniors, or those who need occasional help with shopping or minor household chores. Other volunteers visit nursing homes. If you feel you're not ready to make a long-term commitment, Little Brothers hosts holiday parities and needs help planning, setting up, cleaning, and driving people to and from these events.

Ask the Experts

What's Meals on Wheels, and what do its volunteers do?

These local, independent organizations prepare and deliver hot meals to shut-ins of all ages. These people—particularly the elderly—might not otherwise eat a hot meal or talk to another human being during the day. By delivering meals to them, volunteers not only set up the meal but also assess how the person is doing. (Since the volunteer might be the only outside contact the recipients have, her presence alone is a gift.) Individual volunteers are especially needed in suburban and rural areas to drive delivery trucks or deliver meals. To locate a program near you, visit the Meals on Wheels Association of America (**www.projectmeal.org**) or the National Meals on Wheels Foundation (**www.nationalmealsonwheels.org**).

TURNING POINT

My daughter signed up to deliver Meals on Wheels but backed out when she realized how busy her schedule already was. So she asked me to help. At first I balked—I told her I was 75 and they should be delivering meals to me! But since I had time on my hands, I agreed to pitch in. One of my first clients was a woman who had fallen down and broken her hip. Had I not arrived when I did, she might have remained on the floor for days. Once I realized how important MOW is for "old folks," I got more involved. Within a year I was delivering meals a few days a week and attending volunteer luncheons. I even received a special award for my work.

—Sue R., Vancouver, Washington

prisoners

Becoming better citizens, with your help

Most citizens never consider volunteering at a prison, but inmates need volunteer help too. Often, life skills that most folks take for granted—such as general health and cleanliness and basic personal finance concepts—need to be learned by inmates. And the teachers will almost always be volunteers.

Why volunteer to help people who have committed crimes? By being a good role model for inmates and teaching them skills, you can help them make the move back into society and possibly keep them from becoming repeat offenders. Keep in mind that the environment can range from very intense (high-security penitentiaries) to low-level-security correctional institutions.

If you want to work with younger inmates, get in touch with a local juvenile detention center. If you would prefer to teach, expect to be given some basic orientation to the institution and its inevitable lists of dos and don'ts (you're not allowed to deliver packages for inmates, for instance).

Most prisons have volunteer coordinators. Federal prisons have their own volunteer organization: the Volunteer Management Branch. To find a federal prison near you, or to read the current issue of Volunteer Today (the Bureau of Prisons' official volunteer magazine) visit **www.bop.gov**.

Religion in Prison

Often, prisoners find that their lives are changed when they develop or strengthen their spirituality. Religious organizations of all denominations provide inmates with volunteers who will help nurture inmates of the same religious denomination. While you don't have to be a seminarian to provide this type of work, it is generally important to be well grounded in the basic tenets of your particular religion. Volunteers often develop long-term relationships with inmates and eventually help them make the transition back into the community.

Christianity Prison Fellowship Ministries (**www.pfm.org** or 703-478-0100). PFM volunteers provide one-on-one mentoring, lead bible-study programs, and lead seminars for inmates.

Judaism Jewish Prisoner Services (**www.jewishprisonerservices.org** or 206-985-0577). Provides Jewish publications, pen pals, periodic visitors to Jewish inmates, and support services to their families. This might include observing Passover or High Holidays with them.

Buddhism The Zen Mountain Monastery (**www.mro.org/zmm/prison.htm** or 845-688-2228) has created the National Buddhist Prison Sangha (NBPS), a network of Buddhist volunteers who make themselves available to inmates in their area. These volunteers might write or visit local prisoners or lead religious-practice groups.

You can also contact the American Correctional Chaplains Association at **www.correctional chaplains.org** to find a prison chaplain in your area who might be able to help you find a program that suits your needs.

ASK THE EXPERTS

I want to help, but I'm not sure I'm ready to meet with an inmate face to face yet.

Approach it progressively. Start by simply collecting books and magazines for prisoners. Then consider joining a pen pal program that allows you to communicate with a prisoner through the mail. Eventually, you will probably feel comfortable volunteering in the prison itself. Another way to dip your toe in the water is by helping the Prison Fellowship Ministries' Christmastime Angel Tree ministry. It provides a one-time volunteer opportunity to lift the spirits of a child whose parent is incarcerated by purchasing and delivering gifts to the prisoner's child.

the unemployed

Self-sufficiency and job readiness

Many unemployed and "underemployed" people are hardworking and intelligent individuals who find themselves in a bind. They want to get on their feet but find that the process can be overwhelming. One of the biggest obstacles to employment is simply the interview process: how to get one, what to wear, how to interview. Local organizations can provide instruction in these areas, and volunteers are key to their success.

The Cara Program, for example, is an organization in Chicago that helps motivated homeless people become self-sufficient. Volunteers help participants with their resumés; provide them with computer training; and prepare them for interviews with role-playing exercises. They also match volunteers to mentor program participants. These one-on-one relationships encourage participants as they get back on their feet. Orientation, training, information manuals, and guidance by professional staff are provided to volunteer mentors in these situations.

Life experiences—and simply the desire to help the unemployed—makes most people great mentors.

ASK THE EXPERTS

Which groups work specifically with out-of-work women?

Several national organizations focus on helping low-income women who are looking for work. Among them are Dress for Success (**www.dressforsuccess.org**) and the Women's Alliance (305-762-6400 or **www.thewomensalliance.org**), a group of independent community organizations. Both need volunteers to sort donated work clothes, help clients pick out new clothes, and provide other interviewing and job-placement tips and techniques.

Is there any one-time service I can perform to get my foot in the door and find out if I'll like working with the unemployed?

Yes. A good way to help is to organize a suit drive at your business, school, house of worship, or professional organization. These drives will result in a collection of attractive business clothes that people in need can have for free, enabling them to present a positive impression at a job interview. Your local Dress for Success affiliate (see Web site address above) can provide you with all the necessary instructions and forms. Once your group is on board, simply pick the date, round up friends and co-workers to help out, and notify others when and where to donate their clothes.

I own a small printing company and would like to hire people from these job-readiness organizations. Where should I start?

Contact the Welfare to Work Partnership at **www.welfare to work.org** or 888-872-5621. They help small and medium-sized companies hire and retain employees, and provide mentors for new employees.

the hungry

Harvesting food for the hungry

What is a good way to help the millions of people who go to sleep hungry each night? Most people immediately think of serving at a soup kitchen or a food pantry. That's important work, but it's only part of what needs to be done.

Those in need of food, clothes, and social services can turn to their local community centers. The Community Center of Katonah, New York, which is operated by countless volunteers, has both a food and clothing pantry.

Before you start, understand the big picture of hunger-relief in America—it's broader and more systemic than you might imagine. The nation's largest domestic hunger-relief organization is Second Harvest (**www.secondharvest.org**). This organization solicits food and grocery donations from America's food industry, and distributes the food through their network of over 200 food banks.

The food banks supply more than 50,000 local charitable programs. (That's where your soup kitchens and food pantries come in.) They feed over 26 million hungry Americans (nearly a third of which are children) each year.

Food banks often need volunteers to inspect and sort donated food before it's distributed to local agencies. Volunteers also take food that's been purchased in bulk and repackage it. More hands-on opportunities exist at the delivery level, where the local food pantry is stocked and items are delivered to the needy. Finally, soup kitchens need help with everything from preparing and serving meals to cleaning up, or simply chatting with the visitors as they eat.

ASK THE EXPERTS

What are some one-time services I can perform for the hungry?

Since little training is needed for volunteer positions geared toward the hungry, many offer an unlimited number of one-time opportunities. Contact your local hunger-relief organization or homeless shelter for more information. Find your local food bank or feeding program through **www.secondharvest.org**. You can also find volunteer opportunities through **www.volunteer match.org**, City Cares, Catholic Charities, and United Way.

How do I start a food drive?

It's not as complicated as you might think. In conjunction with your school, employer, or house of worship, simply contact your nearest food bank, which will instruct you on which items it needs the most. Often, the food bank will help you with collection containers, arrange to pick up the donated food, and even provide you with promotional posters and flyers.

Are there particular foods that are in greater demand than others?

Nonperishable staples such as powdered milk and canned foods are always in high demand at most food pantries.

the homeless

A place for the night and hope for the future

Homeless shelters need assistance serving food, helping people move on to gainful employment, or just to provide companionship. Playing cards, sharing a Thanksgiving meal, or reading to children are all possible activities. Some programs need adults to spend the night at the shelter to assist supervisors. There are also many tutoring and mentoring programs available, as well as baby-sitting services that need volunteers.

The National Coalition for the Homeless (**www.nationalhome less.org** or 202-737-6444) can direct you to local volunteer opportunities. Or check the yellow pages for shelters. While there are a number of nonprofit agencies out there to help the homeless, these agencies need volunteers to operate effectively.

Home for Good

What about people who aren't currently homeless, but who need help finding affordable housing? Habitat for Humanity (**www.habitat.org**) uses volunteers to build simple, affordable houses. Don't worry—training is provided. Opportunities also abound for skilled trades, including electricians, plumbers, surveyors, and so on. The families who need shelter pitch in 350 hours of "sweat equity" as their down payment. The families, along with volunteers, work with trained supervisors to construct new housing.

Contact your local Habitat for Humanity for volunteer opportunities in your area. Or, plan a service-oriented vacation: find a habitat building project in the part of the country or world you'd like to visit, and help out while you're away. If you prefer rehabilitating a house, Rebuilding Together (800-473-4229 or **www.christmasinapril.org**) sponsors National Rebuilding Day (also known as Christmas in April) on the last Saturday of April. Volunteers help preserve and revitalize homes for low-income and elderly owners by painting, cleaning, weatherizing, and doing carpentry, plumbing, and electric work.

ASK THE EXPERTS

I'm not sure I want to work directly with the homeless, but I do want to help. What can I do?

Most shelters and other homeless organizations need help for several behind-the-scenes tasks. You might be able to work on an annual fund-raiser, update a Web site, or even serve on a board of directors.

Is there any one-time service I can perform to find out if I'll like working with the homeless?

Coordinating a specific clothing, coat, or blanket drive is a great way to learn about the needs of the homeless and begin interacting with the staff and volunteers of a homeless shelter.

How can I get my house of worship involved?

The National Interfaith Hospitality Networks (NIHN) has helped start up nearly 100 networks of churches and synagogues that provide temporary shelter and meals for homeless families. Call 908-273-1100 or click to **www.nihn.org**. By working with other congregations in your area, your house of worship will periodically be responsible for providing an evening meal, overnight accommodations, breakfast, and a bag lunch for up to 14 guests. Sound like a lot of work? The NIHN will help with start-up considerations, financial issues, volunteer training, board guidance, and more.

disaster relief

Answering the call

When the World Trade Center's twin towers were destroyed on September 11, 2001, nearly every U.S. citizen wanted to help out. Alas, many of the people needed for this type of emergency—and for much smaller-scale disasters—need to be trained before they can pitch in.

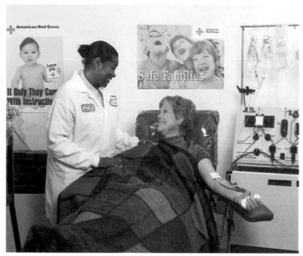

The Red Cross (**www.redcross.org**) and the new Citizen Corps (**www.citizencorps.gov**) encourage volunteers to step up before disaster strikes. The idea is to plan for—and prevent—emergencies and disasters, not just to react to them. If you are interested in becoming a disaster-and-emergency volunteer, you'll start by serving in your own community. Everyday disasters, including home and apartment fires or severe floods, need compassionate neighbors to step forward to help shelter and feed people who suddenly find themselves homeless.

Once you've been trained and have served locally, you might want to be a part of the national teams that fly all over the country to help out in larger emergencies—often at a moment's notice. But it's not so easy to join in. Only volunteers who have undergone the high-quality training that prepares them for all situations—and gives them the confidence they need—are eligible.

Much disaster-relief work is already going on behind the scenes before it's needed. By volunteering to help out in some capacity, you will receive training, learn the ropes, and be ready when disaster strikes.

ASK THE EXPERTS

What do relief workers do?

You might be surprised at the wide range of duties that are performed before, during, and after a disaster. Besides filling sandbags during a flood, volunteers work with displaced families to find them food and shelter. They might pour cold drinks for firefighters. Doctors and nurses are needed to provide healthcare services to the wounded. Mental health professionals are needed to work with traumatized victims.

I'm nervous about working on-site after a disaster has struck. Are other types of work available?

There are a number of ways that you can help out behind the scenes. Be part of the logistics group that contacts the local school or church to find sleeping facilities for families without homes. Determine how to quickly find cots, blankets, water, and food. Be part of the human resource group that tracks what staff and volunteers are doing at all times. Donate your administrative skills by transcribing disaster plans or gathering and getting facilities agreements signed.

now what do I do?
Answers to common questions

How can I help people who suffer from drug abuse?

To work directly with drug abusers, you generally need to be a trained professional. But you can offer assistance to one of the many drug abuse/prevention organizations with fund-raising, administrative work, or other behind-the-scenes activities. Also, mentoring has proven to be a highly effective way to help prevent drug abuse. Even if you never talk about it directly, underprivileged kids with mentors are less likely to abuse drugs than those without.

Are there any short-term projects I can participate in to see if working with senior citizens is right for me?

Most Meals on Wheels programs receive enough federal funds to provide only one hot meal to recipients Monday through Friday, excluding holidays. As a result, many Meals on Wheels organizations have developed a separately funded holiday program that provides meals on holidays. You can help them by taking tickets at a fund-raiser (they don't receive federal funds for this program) or by offering to deliver meals on a holiday. This is a great way to see if you'd like to get more involved.

If there is a local disaster, what are the most immediate ways to assist victims?

Start by calling your local fire or police department. If there is a safety issue, be prepared to be told to stay put and out of danger. It doesn't help to have volunteers running around in a hurricane or a fire. Once the danger has passed, the fire or police department will need volunteers to help provide food and clothing. If you know of your immediate neighbors who are in need, seek them out and offer your assistance.

What is a grocery bag purchase program?

It's a program that lets you donate food to others as you shop. Many major food retailers make available special grocery bags that you fill with food for the needy as you shop for yourself. After you've paid for the bag of food at the checkout, the retailer arranges for the food to be donated to a local shelter or pantry. Ask your store if it has such a program.

Now where do I go!

CONTACTS

Red Cross
877-272-7337
www.redcross.org

**National Voluntary Organizations
Active in Disaster (NVOAD)**
www.nvoad.org

Points of Light
800-865-8683
www.volunteerconnections.org

City Cares
404-875-7334
www.citycares.org

National Coalition for the Homeless
202-737-6444
www.nationalhomeless.org

Habitat for Humanity
www.habitat.org

**National Coalition
Against Domestic Violence**
303-839-1852
www.ncadv.org

Child Welfare League of America
262-638-2952
www.cwla.org

Second Harvest
www.secondharvest.org

BOOKS

Volunteering to Help in Your Neighborhood
By Claudia Isler

Volunteering to Help Seniors
By Patrick Newell

**Helping Battered Women:
A Volunteer's Handbook**
By Alan W. McEvoy and Jeff B. Brookings

**Helping Battered Women:
New Perspectives and Remedies**
By Albert R. Roberts (Editor)

**The Prison Minister's Handbook: Volunteer
Ministry to the Forgotten Christian**
By John Cowart

**Lighting the Way: Volunteer Child
Advocates Speak Out**
By the Child Welfare League of America

**Habitat for Humanity: Building Private Homes,
Building Public Religion**
By Jerome P. Baggett

54 Ways You Can Help the Homeless
By Rabbi Charles A. Kroloff

6

Health

Beyond medicine, volunteers offer smiles, give comfort, and lift spirits.

the importance of health volunteers

Religious orders established hospitals as early as the Middle Ages to care for the sick and dying. While plagues, leprosy, and significantly shorter life expectancies made volunteer opportunities plentiful many centuries ago, volunteers fill a new void today. With the cost of care skyrocketing, hospital and other medical staff are dwindling, and the workers who remain are under tremendous stress. In many cases, it's the volunteers who are able to help out with the "warm and fuzzy" aspect of medical treatment that professional caregivers no longer have the luxury of providing to their patients.

What motivates these volunteers? In many cases, they themselves have been touched by a personal health issue. A breast cancer survivor might offer to help in an organization that raises funds to find a cure; a parent who has lost a child might volunteer in a children's hospital to comfort other grieving parents; someone who's married to a doctor or nurse might understand the pressures facing medical professionals and volunteer in a hospital to help care for patients. And since such folks have firsthand experience, they're able to donate more than their time. They bring a special compassion and empathy to those they are serving.

Whether you're working directly with the ill, fund-raising for a cure, or doing administrative tasks, the work is important in that it has a real effect on people's health and happiness.

ASK THE EXPERTS

How can I donate blood?

Visit **www.givelife.org** or call 800-448-3543. As long as you're at least 17 years old, healthy, weigh 110 pounds, and haven't donated in the last 56 days, you may be eligible.

Is there any way to work with disabled veterans?

There are numerous ways to help disabled vets, from such simple tasks as delivering mail at VA hospitals to helping vets write letters to providing companionship, especially around the holidays. You can also help them have fun by passing out name tags at a bass-fishing or trapshooting event or keeping score at a disabled vets basketball game. Contact the Paralyzed Veterans of America at 800-424-8200 or **www.pva.org** or the Disabled American Veterans at 859-441-7300 or **www.dav.org**. Both have local chapters that provide a variety of services to our vets.

How do I know if volunteering in the health field is a good fit for me?

That's a good question. First consider your comfort level with disease. Health volunteers need to be fairly comfortable dealing with people who are either ill or have a deformity or disability. Some people become volunteers because they experienced some health-related problems and want to help others.

your local hospital

By lending their hands and their hearts, volunteers provide relief to sick patients, concerned visitors, and weary hospital staff 24 hours a day, 7 days a week, 365 days a year. In fact, nonprofit hospitals (charity hospitals that can receive tax-exempt funding) are required to have a certain number of volunteers on staff or else they jeopardize their nonprofit status. For-profit hospitals also need volunteers, but not to such an extent.

What types of volunteer jobs are available? All sorts. You can deliver flowers or mail to patients, give out books and newspapers, play games with pediatric patients, or help the family members of gravely ill patients.

You're not expected to be a health expert. Whether you want to bring your pet and provide animal-assisted therapy or volunteer in the intensive care unit to update and support anxious family members, there are training programs that teach basic hospital procedures, rules and regulations, plus whatever you'll need to know for your specific volunteer position.

You may also have to go through a rigorous screening process before being allowed to volunteer. It's not unusual to be asked to interview, supply references, pass a criminal background check, agree to volunteer a minimum number of hours, pass a health screening test, and stick to the organization's dress code.

Because of the volunteer's vital importance to nonprofit hospitals, the hospitals have full-time volunteer coordinators to help potential volunteers get started. Simply call your local hospital or look for volunteer information on hospital Web sites.

ASK THE EXPERTS

I hear that most hospitals require extensive commitments from their volunteers. True?

Sometimes. Because of the time spent in training volunteers, most hospitals want to make sure their volunteers are serious about their commitment. That being said, there are sometimes special events or periodic volunteer opportunities that might suit your needs. If a regular commitment is required, however, you'll probably have the choice of evenings, weekends, or daytime hours.

I'm not sure I would feel comfortable working directly with patients. Is there any other way I can help?

Like most service organizations, hospitals need help in the gift shop or cafeteria, at the information desk, or with organization, clerical work, and fund-raising. And if you're interested in education, you'll be pleased to learn that most hospitals need docents to provide tours to hospital visitors and school groups.

Five Common Hospital Volunteer Positions

Family support Tend to family needs in surgical areas, waiting areas, and intensive care units by delivering snacks, gift baskets, or reading material. Sit with hospitalized loved ones so family members can take a break.

Gift shop These stores help support hospital programs and services, and therefore play an important role. Help with daily operations, merchandise displays, inventory, and customer sales.

Patient support Play cards and games with patients; deliver flowers, mail, or books; give massages; or simply visit bedridden patients.

Information desk Greet patients and visitors, provide general hospital information and directions, and field telephone calls.

Doctor/nurse support Deliver water, towels, and linens to patients; answer patients' call lights; take patients for walks; escort them to the exits via wheelchair when they are discharged; help feed elderly or infant patients.

children's hospitals

A big hand for little ones

While most hospitals provide volunteer opportunities to work with kids, consider volunteering at a children's hospital if you really want to focus on helping youngsters. More than simply a hospital that specializes in pediatrics, children's hospitals are kid-friendly and child-size, and actually benefit all children by pioneering research for vaccinations, training the majority of pediatricians, and actively educating the public about healthcare and injury prevention.

How can volunteers help? In addition to doing any of the routine things needed in a hospital (see page 108), you might find yourself cuddling and rocking abandoned babies, playing board games with a teenage cancer patient, or reading to a youngster who is waiting for an X ray. Playrooms need volunteers to help the staff supervise activities and games. Some children's hospitals provide pet therapy, in which children play with pets brought in by volunteers.

To protect the children's safety and well-being, the screening process for potential volunteers is often stricter than at regular hospitals. For more information, contact the volunteer coordinator for your local children's hospital, or check out its Web site.

The Shriners

Established by the Shrine, an auxiliary of the Masons, the first Shriners children's hospital opened in 1922. Today there are 22 of these specialty hospitals that help children with severe orthopedic or burn injuries, regardless of a family's ability to pay.

ASK THE EXPERTS

I'd like to volunteer with a group of my friends. Are there any children-oriented charities that could use our help?

Ronald McDonald Houses have plenty of opportunities for group volunteering. If there's a chef among you, you can sign up to cook a buffet-style meal for the 25 or so guests at the house. And if you enjoy the experience, you can do it as often as once a month. There are also occasional cleaning or maintenance projects that need groups of helpers.

What is the Make-A-Wish Foundation?

The Make-A-Wish Foundation at **www.wish.org** or 800-722-WISH (9474) and similar organizations make special wishes come true for children with life-threatening illnesses. Once you voice your preferences and pass the application and screening process, you'll be assigned to a volunteer position. If you're chosen for a wish-granting position, you'll work as a pair with another wish granter from start to finish. This involves meeting with the child and the child's family, uncovering the wish (which is not always easy),

Raquel, age 10, wished to swim with the dolphins.

and working with the office staff and other resources to make the sick child's wish come true. You'll also help deliver the wish, whether it's accompanying the child on a shopping spree or driving him to the airport to meet the pope. While the wish-granting position might sound great, it can be hard to get, and it's a lot of work. Equally, if not more important—and often a better place to start—are the many other support volunteer positions, like helping to organize travel and medical arrangements for the wish recipient, as well as the standard nonprofit needs.

What is a Ronald McDonald House?

A Ronald McDonald House (**www.rmhc.org/home/index.html**) is a low-cost/no-cost "home-away-from-home" for families with seriously ill kids who are staying in nearby hospitals. Volunteers are needed to greet and check in families as they arrive, tidy up around the house, and answer the house phone. Also needed are weekend managers to work one weekend a month—from Friday night until Sunday night—to oversee the house. The weekend manager is provided with a private bedroom.

people with disabilities

Rehabilitation or recreation

Maybe your life has been touched by a sudden, disabling accident. Or perhaps a loved one has cerebral palsy or some other developmental disability. Whatever the motivation, deciding to volunteer to help the physically, mentally, or emotionally disabled offers tremendous rewards.

You can either work with individuals one-on-one or serve the organizations that support them, such as Easter Seals or Disabled American Veterans. Most of these advocacy groups need help providing education, advocacy, support groups, and a myriad of other services (for more on advocacy, see pages 34–35). If you want to help people with a specific disability, find and contact an organization that serves that population and talk with their volunteer coordinator.

What types of jobs would a volunteer do? Among the many, you can help an instructor teach a group of disabled adults how to silk-screen; lead horses for autistic children attending a therapeutic horseback-riding session; or simply transport a disabled person to a doctor's appointment. The opportunities are endless.

If you want to be a friend to someone with Down's syndrome or another intellectual disability, join Best Buddies.

ASK THE EXPERTS

I'd like to work with disabled kids. Where should I start?

Your local Easter Seals headquarters might be a good place. This group serves children with cerebral palsy, Down's syndrome, autism, and other developmental disabilities. Besides fund-raising and other typical volunteer opportunities, they have therapeutic classrooms, special-needs childcare facilities, and Head Start programs that allow volunteers to lend a hand. Contact the program manager at your local office for details. To learn more, call 800-221-6827 or click to **www.easter-seals.org**.

What are Independent Living Centers?

Independent Living Centers, of which there are more than 500, are independent, nonprofit, community-based organizations that provide a variety of services to the disabled to help them reach their potential in their families and communities. The centers help with housing, employment, transportation, health, recreational, and social issues. (Note: The people served do not live at the center.) To contact an Independent Living Center near you, go online to their Web site: **www.ilusa.com**.

How do I sign up to just hang out and be friends with a disabled person in need?

Best Buddies (**www.bestbuddies.org**) pairs up students and local citizens with people with mental retardation for one-to-one friendships. In the best interest of both friends, Best Buddies facilitates and monitors each friendship. Call 800-892-8339 to see if there's a group in your area.

TURNING POINT

After being let go from my job in advertising, I was depressed and needed a healthy outlet. I began helping my local Easter Seals headquarters with some routine office work. One day my supervisor told me they desperately needed some help in one of their classrooms—one of their volunteer teacher's aides left unexpectedly. I was scared. Never having been exposed to kids with disabilities, I didn't know what to expect, and I wasn't sure how to interact with them. When I got there, the teacher introduced me to each child and explained a little bit about each one. As I began to understand and appreciate each of these children, and felt more comfortable with each, I realized how much I enjoyed helping them. As a result, I went back to school and am now a full-time special education teacher—and loving it.

—Gerald B., Richardson, Texas

hospice

Dignity for the dying

Hospices were introduced to the United States in the mid-1960s, when Dame Cicely Sanders, the founder of a hospice in London, visited Yale University and shared a new method of caring for people in the terminal stage of an illness.

By creating a more homelike environment and letting family members be on hand with their dying relative, hospice care helped both patient and loved ones cope with the inevitable death. The first hospice opened in 1974, and there are now over 3,100 hospice programs in the U.S.

Volunteers can care for patients by keeping them company and by reading to them, listening to them, or even running errands or doing shopping. Family members are also comforted by volunteers, who stay with the patient when the family member needs to take a break. Volunteers also provide emotional support, transportation, and even childcare.

Once the patient has passed on, volunteers can continue to serve, supporting the bereaved loved ones through letters, telephone calls, or home visits, or by facilitating membership in a support group. If you feel unprepared for such work, most hospices have training for volunteers, which may run from 20 to 40 hours. The training generally covers a variety of topics, including what death and illness means to the dying person and to his family, listening skills, how to care for patients, and how to interact with the family.

If you prefer to support the hospice without working directly with those affected, you can serve your local hospice by speaking at health fairs and other community events to raise awareness and funds (see page 35).

ASK THE EXPERTS

Where does hospice care take place?

It depends. Some hospices have stand-alone facilities, hospitals often have hospice units, and sometimes the care is given in the patient's home. Visit **www.hospicefoundation.org**, check your local yellow pages, or call 800-854-3402 to find a hospice near you.

What is respite care?

Respite care is simply giving family members a break (or respite) from caring for a sick loved one. Staying attentive to a dying relative can be stressful, so volunteers who provide this care to family members allow them to "recharge their batteries" while ensuring that the dying patient is not left alone. Dying alone is one of the biggest fears of those approaching the end of life.

fighting disease

Preventive medicine

The prevention, treatment, and cure of specific diseases is the goal of nonprofit organizations that fund research, raise awareness, and support victims of the respective sicknesses. Fund-raising for research is often the top priority of these disease-focused organizations.

Whether you're organizing a celebrity golf outing, asking corporations to donate items for a silent auction, or just selling raffle tickets at a gala dinner, you'll be having fun while you're helping out. By collecting pledges and following through, you'll help raise money for the group, awareness of the disease, and—in the event of a charity walk or jog—your heart rate!

Other volunteer jobs include helping to educate the public about these diseases. A number of disease-fighting organizations use volunteers to answer hot lines; distribute information; provide literature to local hospitals and doctors; and give talks at local schools, businesses, and community centers.

Fund-Raising to Fight Disease

The Leukemia & Lymphoma Society's Team in Training allows volunteers to combine fund-raising with fun. In return for raising a certain amount of money (usually a few thousand dollars or so) from sponsors, you will receive everything you need to participate in the athletic event of your dreams: running a marathon in Hawaii or in Ireland, or doing a triathlon in California. You'll not only get 16 weeks of supervised training (twice a week) but also get airfare, lodging in a four-star hotel, and team dinners before and after the event. You'll even be assigned a personal mentor to help you with all the preparations. To learn more, visit **www.teamintraining.org**. A similar program, Joints in Motion, is sponsored by the Arthritis Foundation (**www.arthritis.org**).

Their Specialties

Many disease-focused organizations have their own foundations. Some are quite large, with many different offices or branches. Depending on the organization, you can volunteer to work directly with people who suffer from these diseases by leading support groups or visiting with sick individuals; or you can help out in fund-raising and awareness efforts.

American Cancer Society
800-227-2345
www.cancer.org

Arthritis Foundation
800-283-7800
www.arthritis.org

American Heart Association
800-242-8721
www.americanheart.org

National Multiple Sclerosis Society
800-344-4867
www.nmss.org

American Diabetes Association
800-342-2383
www.diabetes.org

Parkinson's Disease Foundation
800-457-6676
www.pdf.org

Alzheimer's Association
800-272-3900
www.alz.org

American Lung Association
212-315-8700
www.lungusa.org

now what do I do?
Answers to common questions

How can I get involved with groups like the Special Olympics?

There are many sports organizations that rely on volunteers like you to help the disabled enjoy recreational activities. Contact any of the following: Special Olympics International (**www.specialolympics.org**); Disabled Sports USA (**www.dsusa.org**); USA Deaf Sports Federation (**www.usadsf.org**); Wheelchair Sports USA (**www.wsusa.org**); United States Cerebral Palsy Athletic Association (**www.uscpaa.org**); or Association of Blind Athletes (**www.usaba.org**).

I'm interested in working with people who are paralyzed or who have suffered spinal cord injuries. What opportunities are there?

In addition to helping paralyzed vets or supporting wheelchair sports (see above), many opportunities exist at rehabilitation hospitals. Although some programs limit volunteer contact with those with severe disabilities, others welcome your help with feeding and transporting patients. You can also help a patient with his physical or occupational therapy or take him to recreational activities like weekend baseball games.

What groups work with the blind?

Many local organizations serve the needs of the blind and the visually impaired. They look for volunteers who will read mail to the blind, take them grocery shopping, write letters for them, and make recordings of books or articles on tape. The first place to start is your local Lighthouse for the Blind organization. Call 800-829-0500 or click to **www.light house.org** to find your local organization.

How can I get involved in helping people with cerebral palsy?

Contact Volunteers in Health Care at **www.volunteersinhealthcare.org** or call them at 877-844-8442. United Cerebral Palsy (**www.ucpa.org**) also needs help with special events, fund-raising, and answering phones for a telethon. Its mission is to help people with CP and other disabilities live independent, productive lives.

What if I want to volunteer in the area of mental-health care?

When it comes to mental-health care, volunteers are needed to help with everything from substance abuse to depression to post-traumatic stress disorder. Opportunities range from wrapping holiday presents for the mentally ill, to educating the public about mental illness, to serving food at a fund-raiser, to leading a support group. Contact the National Mental Health Organization (**www.nmha.org**) to find your local affiliate. You can also contact the National Alliance for the Mentally Ill (NAMI), the largest grassroots organization that helps people with mental disorders, and their friends and families. If you have a loved one with a severe mental illness, you can teach in NAMI's Family to Family program. After taking an intensive training program, you'll teach a 12-week class to other concerned family members. Reach them at 703-524-7600 or visit **www.nami.org**.

Now where do I go!

CONTACTS

Make-A-Wish Foundation
800-722-9474
www.wish.org
Grants special requests from children
with life-threatening illnesses.

Volunteer Match
www.volunteermatch.org
Internet clearinghouse for volunteer positions.

United Way
www.unitedway.org

Paralyzed Veterans of America
800-424-8200
www.pva.org

Disabled American Veterans
859-441-7300
www.dav.org

Mobility International USA
www.miusa.org
Empowers people with disabilities.

Easter Seals
800-221-6827
www.easter-seals.org
Helping disabled children.

Hospice Foundation
800-854-3402
www.hospicefoundation.org

BOOKS

**Horse the Handicapped, the Riding Team
in a Therapeutic Riding Program:
A Volunteer Training Manual**
By Barbara T. Engel (Editor)

**When Evening Comes:
The Education of a Hospice Volunteer**
By Christine Andreae

**Volunteering With Your Pet: How to Get
Involved in Animal-Assisted Therapy With Any
Kind of Pet (paperback edition, Wanted:
Animal Volunteers)**
By Mary R. Burch

7
Educational opportunities

Volunteering at a school can make the difference between mediocrity and excellence.

volunteering in schools

Ready to go back to school?

If you have children—and even if you don't—it's hard not to notice that our schools need help. Teachers and administrators from preschools to high schools (public and private alike) are strained as never before. Financial resources are tight, and so is the time most potential volunteers have to help out. Still, many find a way, knowing that volunteering at a school can help make the difference between mediocrity and excellence.

Take a few minutes to consider your local school's needs, and chances are good that you'll find a match for your interests and skills. Maybe you have a passion for music or plays and like the idea of volunteering a few hours a week to help the drama coach produce a school play. Or perhaps you're a computer whiz, in which case your skills would come in handy when the school needs to upgrade its computers.

You can volunteer at a school to be a chaperone for a student field trip.

If you want to work in the classroom, you can volunteer to help a teacher. You can either take on a one-time project with the kids or help on a weekly basis. If you choose the latter, you'll act as a volunteer teacher's aide, responsible for things as varied as helping a struggling child keep up with the rest of the class, cleaning up after an art project, and helping to plan and coordinate such activities as a Valentine's Day party or a field trip.

How do you start? Go to the office of a local school and ask them what they need. They should then direct you to the local group that provides them with volunteers. Some school districts will even have a volunteer coordinator.

ASK THE EXPERTS

The school wants to run a background check on me. Is that unusual?

Most schools and other child-oriented organizations require background checks for their weekly volunteers, even if the volunteers are parents. Don't take this personally; as advocates for children, they're simply looking out for the children's best interests. Since it can be costly to run a check on every volunteer, some organizations will ask you to pay the fee for a background check. Some other schools forgo background checks and opt for letters of recommendation from friends or coworkers.

I own a small business in the area. How can I help the local school?

While volunteering your own time is certainly worthwhile, volunteering your business's resources in a partnership with the school can actually be more effective. For instance, if you own an advertising agency, you could offer to help the school publicize its fund-raising events. Or you and the school might agree to create an after-school homework program that has your staff members as volunteers. Besides boosting your employees' morale, pitching in at the school might even help boost your business.

Do school libraries need help?

Yes. School libraries need help with everything from checking in and shelving books to filling in for the librarian. They also need help with fund-raising. If you have computer skills, consider volunteering at your library's multimedia center.

parent/teacher groups

Working together

Founded in 1897, the Parent Teacher Association (PTA) is a national nonprofit membership organization that serves as an advocate for all children. The idea behind the PTA is to help schools and parents work more effectively together in helping children succeed. Individuals can join a local PTA for a small fee or start a unit through their state PTA. A parent/teacher organization (PTO) is simply a generic term used by any school's independent parent/teacher organization. Both the PTA and a PTO are independent from the school and are run completely by volunteers.

The kind of help the PTA and PTO seek out depends on your school's strengths and its needs. Most organizations have a variety of committees that call for both leaders and helpers. The welcoming committee might host a new-teacher luncheon; the playground committee might review the school's equipment and suggest improvements; the yearbook committee will help the students fund and produce their yearbook.

These groups also need representatives to work within the community to help stretch the school's limited funds. For instance, the head of a PTO arts committee might ask the local Lions Club to sponsor the school play.

If it all seems a little daunting, just take a deep breath and start by attending a meeting and see what happens. You'll learn more about your school's parent/teacher group and its goals and needs once you get involved.

ASK THE EXPERTS

What if my school doesn't have a PTA or PTO group?

If your school doesn't have a parent/teacher organization, why not start one? Check out **www.pta.org** or **www.ptotoday.com** for information, plus advice about how to proceed. (See more in Chapter 11.)

Can I help out even if I don't have children in the school?

Yes! The only requirement to join these organizations is a sincere desire to help; you don't have to be a relative of students or teachers.

I've been asked to be on a PTO's fund-raising committee. What should I expect?

Expect to be busy. As school budgets get squeezed, parents and administrators look for creative ways to fill the gaps. In a day when schools are forced to make test-score performance a top priority, funds for computers in the classrooms, new uniforms for the volleyball team, and new playground equipment for recess often take a back seat. In the past, a simple PTO bake sale or car wash would fill the gap. Now school fund-raising is a virtual industry. Schools sell everything from candles to cookie dough to cookbooks consisting of parents' favorite recipes. Volunteers are needed in every step of the process—from organizing and directing the entire project to simply staffing a candy-sale table during a football game. (For more on fundraising, see page 203.)

joining a board of education

Just like regular and nonprofit corporations, school districts need boards of directors (see pages 44–45). What exactly does a board of education do? Many, many things. They are the backbone of the public school system. In essence, the board of education sets goals and visions for its school district.

Education boards typically consist of five or seven members, who serve three- to four-year terms. In some states, these positions are appointed by the governor or mayor or a special convention; in other states, board members are voted into office.

One major function of the board is to prepare the annual school budget and decide how money is spent. Since many school district budgets can run into the hundreds of millions of dollars, this is a huge responsibility. But don't worry— board members can attend periodic conferences which offer training in budgets and the budgeting process.

Many boards have subcommittees made up of board members and community volunteers to help divvy up the work and report back to board members. The facilities committee, for example, works with each school's facilities director to review what capital improvements need to be made (a new roof, for example), or even whether two schools should be consolidated into one. A policy committee sets the district's policies and regulations. Committee members might decide how the actual school buildings can be used after school hours, which groups are eligible to use the facilities, and how much to charge for using them. Finally, the legislation committee might analyze proposed local, state, and federal laws and work on influencing local representatives to cast votes that will ultimately benefit children and schools.

ASK THE EXPERTS

I've been asked to run for our local board of education, but I'm worried about the time commitment. Should I be?

Like all volunteer jobs, you need to assess your availability and be up front about how much time you can commit. Besides weekly or biweekly meetings (which could take up to 20 hours a month), you'll probably be required to participate in subcommittees and field phone calls from parents, students, and teachers. There are some fun perks—you get to represent the board at year-end sports banquets, retirement dinners, and graduations.

Will I incur expenses as a school board member?

Most likely yes, but they should be covered by your school district. Some districts offer their board members a modest annual stipend to help defray costs like travel, telephone, and faxing. Others have expense-reimbursement procedures that will enable you to recoup your costs.

I hear that being a school board member can be demanding. Is this true?

That depends on what you consider demanding. There is the time commitment to consider as well as the fact that you will be asked to make decisions that impact the health and well-being of your school district. You may find yourself at loggerheads with other board members over key issues, such as budgets, textbooks, and course selection. Or you may find that your fellow board members share your concerns and goals. Just know that any debate you have is part of the democratic process that makes for a well-run school district.

mentoring

Disadvantaged youths who have had mentors are less likely to do drugs or get into fights. Better still, they are more likely to stay in school and go to college. What is a mentor? It's a grown-up who agrees to guide a youth who needs help navigating life's rocky roads. Being a positive role model, and showing that you care, can make a world of difference to a child.

Programs like Big Brothers Big Sisters of America match disadvantaged children with adult volunteer mentors. Here, mentors meet once or twice a week with the assigned kids, simply talking or hanging out or taking in a movie. And mentoring doesn't just mean working with the disadvantaged. For nearly 100 years, Boy Scout and Girl Scout troop leaders have been helping turn boys and girls from all walks of life into better citizens.

Bring a little magic into your own life, and the life of a child, by sharing experiences that build memories and friendship. That's what being a Big Brother or Big Sister is all about.

Mentors often say that the satisfaction they gain from volunteering exceeds their wildest expectations. There is nothing more rewarding than watching young people who were previously involved with drugs or gangs going off to college or getting their first jobs—or even becoming mentors themselves.

ASK THE EXPERTS

How can I find out more about mentoring?

Getting involved with mentoring is easy. Just contact Big Brothers Big Sisters (**www.bbbsa.org** or 215-567-7000), or the Boys & Girls Clubs (**www.bgca.org** or 404-487-5700). You can also visit **www.mentoring.org** and enter your zip code for a mentoring opportunity near you. Volunteer centers, City Cares, Americorps, and the United Way also provide ample mentoring opportunities.

How can I get involved with scouting groups?

These groups always need volunteers. The Girl Scouts of America, for instance, needs troop leaders who plan and supervise the weekly meetings. But they also need help with one-time volunteer events (like handing out information about free health insurance for needy kids) or sharing professional knowledge to help girls earn badges for everything from engineering to nursing. If you want to get involved with scouting, contact the Boy Scouts and Cub Scouts (**www.scouting.org**—or call your local council), or the Girl Scouts and Brownies (**www.girlscouts.org** or 800-478-7248).

I very much want to be a mentor, but I live in a pretty remote area. Any suggestions?

Online mentoring might be the answer, and visiting **www.serviceleader.org/vv/forvols.html** will let you explore online opportunities. Just keep in mind most of them require an initial face-to-face meeting or two with the person you'll be mentoring. Other online opportunities are available only through participating companies.

TURNING POINT

I was reluctant to get involved in my 6-year-old's Brownie activities, much less become the troop leader. After all, I was a shy, stay-at-home mom who never went to college. What could I offer these girls? My daughter convinced me to sign on, and I bloomed! The change started with my training, where I learned about everything from conflict resolution, to camping, to cookie sales. Before long, I had worked my way up to volunteer communications coordinator, and was creating and sending out press releases, being interviewed on TV, and even networking with the media.

—Nancy F., Scottsdale, Arizona

tutoring

Working one-on-one

Children who receive tutoring not only get a better grasp of subjects but gain self-confidence. (Tutoring is especially helpful to those kids who are too intimidated to ask questions in a 30-student classroom.) No one expects a tutor to know it all, but rather to act as a homework coach and a trusted adult confidant.

Before you start tutoring, you may have to undergo some training yourself. After all, tutoring is more than simply helping students solve algebra problems—it's about helping them learn algebra well enough so that they can solve the problems independently. Tutors also must provide information that's consistent with the school curriculum and the teacher's approach to it.

As with other child-related volunteer opportunities, expect background checks. Depending on the program, you might also need to meet certain educational requirements or be interviewed.

If $a = 4$ and $b = 4$ then $a = b$

$5n + 2n = 7n$

ASK THE EXPERTS

How can I start tutoring?

Tutoring programs are plentiful. Contact your local YMCA
(**www.ymca.net** or 312-977-0031) or Boys & Girls Clubs
(**www.bgca.org** or 404-487-5700) or your local public library.
You can also get involved through your local volunteer center,
City Cares, or by approaching your local school directly.

I want to be with my kids after school and at night, but I'd still like to tutor. Are there any other options?

Some schools bring in daytime tutors to help kids during
study hall or free periods. Check with your school or your local
tutoring program to see if tutoring during school hours is
allowed. If not, ask your school if you can start a program!

What is a typical tutoring session like?

All tutoring sessions are different, depending on the child's
age, whether you focus on one subject or many, and whether you
help with homework or supply supplemental information. That
being said, it's good to start a tutoring session by simply chatting
and seeing how your student is doing. Because the child's mood
can affect your session, it's always good to know how she's feeling and whether anything significant happened in school that
day. Next, recap what you did last week and test her with a few
sample questions to gauge her progress; this tells you whether to
move forward or stay with last week's material. Soon, you'll gain
a sense of how fast to proceed. Your pupil will probably get frustrated if you stay on a subject that she's uncomfortable with.
Interjecting short games can help alleviate boredom, and you
also could also end each session with a game—a quick round of
tick-tack-toe, perhaps.

literacy

Read all about it

If you think that "literacy volunteering" just means teaching people to read, think again. The Literacy Volunteers of America (LVA) defines adult literacy as the ability to read, write, and speak English proficiently, plus the ability to compute and solve problems and use technology. Combined, these skills enable a person to become a lifelong learner and to interact effectively in the family, the workplace, and the community. To this end, LVA also conducts classes in English as a second language, to help those who didn't grow up speaking it.

Literacy programs in prisons have proved to bring down repeat-offender rates. And while most children with illiterate parents struggle to read, kids with parents who have been through literacy programs often "break the cycle" of illiteracy.

If you're interested in literacy but don't want to work one-on-one, you can volunteer to be a teacher's aide in an adult literacy class. Other opportunities include liter-acy awareness programs, book give-aways, and special reading events.

Literacy tutoring programs are typically geared toward either children or adults, and some literacy programs require extensive training. Programs affiliated with the Literacy Volunteers of America, for example, require an 18-hour training course.

ASK THE EXPERTS

How can I get hooked up with a literacy program?

Many literacy programs originate at your local library, so get in touch with their volunteer coordinator for details. You can also contact Literacy Volunteers of America (**www.literacyvolunteers.org**), the Internet service **www.volunteermatch.org**, or your local volunteer center. The National Institute for Literacy (800-228-8813) will also refer you to local volunteer programs focused on literacy.

What is Reading is FUNdamental?

Reading is FUNdamental (RIF) has a National Book Program that gives books to kids—especially those who might not have books at home. Volunteers are needed to choose and order books, dress as a character and read books aloud, or fill an administrative position. Call 877-743-7323 or visit **www.rif.org**.

I'm so squeezed for time these days, my lunch hour is the only time I have available. Are there any lunchtime volunteer opportunities?

Try a Power Lunch, a lunchtime literacy program sponsored by certain corporations that pairs students with adult employees. Contact Everybody Wins at **www.everybodywins.org** or 212-966-4677.

Some of my coworkers also want to help with literacy. Can we organize something as a group?

Become a Literacy Volunteers of America Workplace Advocate. They'll coach you on how to talk to your employer about becoming partners with your local LVA program, allowing you and your co-workers to provide regular tutoring or help with a one-time literacy event. (Visit **www.literacyvolunteers.org** or call 315-472-0001.) Or you might consider creating a workplace literacy program, in which volunteers team up with companies located in areas with large immigrant populations. The goal is to teach rudimentary English to employees so they can read—especially warning signs such as "Danger" or "Do not mix these chemicals together."

arts education

Creative opportunities

Tight budgets and increasing pressure for high test scores have forced many public and private schools to cut back on art, music, and drama programs. What to do? Volunteer to do whatever you can to fix the problem. There are numerous ways to help: In some classrooms, you could teach kids how to finger paint, play the French horn, identify and cut out magazine pictures for collage projects, or simply help teachers clean up after art projects. One industrious mom in Skokie, Illinois, volunteered to choreograph, direct, and supervise the production of *Swan Lake* for her daughter's entire 5th grade class, while other parents chipped in to make the costumes, supervise rehearsals, and act as stage hands. (For more on how to start your own volunteer project, see pages 194–211.)

By raising money, heightening awareness, and lending a hand, parents and community members can make sure schoolchildren's access to the arts doesn't vanish.

A St. Louis student paints a mural in an art residency program with Young Audiences artist Robert Ketchens.

ASK THE EXPERTS

How do I get involved with arts education?

Your local PTA or PTO—or the school itself—can help you get involved in the arts, whether it's helping with direct hands-on art activities, fund-raising, or advocacy. You might also contact your state arts council or local park district for ways to get involved. Or contact Young Audiences, the oldest and largest organization in the country for getting the arts into local schools. To find one of their 32 chapters, visit their Web site at **www.youngaudiences.org** or call 800-836-0494.

I've been asked to help raise money for the marching band. How can I go about it?

Since inadequate funding is the root cause of many art program crises, fund-raising is a vital way to help the arts. More money is always needed—and not only for marching band uniforms but for art supplies and drama department productions. Turn your creativity loose on the fund-raising world. Fund-raising can be as simple as a local bake sale or as complex as Portland's annual Run for the Arts, a citywide fund-raiser and awareness campaign that included participation from the mayor and Trailblazer players—and raised $500,000.

athletics

Play ball

If you love sports, combine your passion for recreation with your desire to volunteer. You may find some volunteer opportunities in your local school's sports program—as a timekeeper, perhaps, or a scorekeeper. If you prefer coaching, then consider your youth sports teams; here, volunteer jobs are usually filled by parents of children who play on the team. It's a demanding position, but it can be a lot of fun.

Training for new coaches has become increasingly popular. For example, the Little League Organization (**www.littleleague.org**) has a variety of manuals, guides, videos, and CD's that help train managers and coaches. You'll learn how to work with kids, the basics of competition and sportsmanship, and how to handle difficult situations. (Note: Public schools can entrust coaching positions only to those who have a teaching certificate, and assistant coaching positions are often filled by recent college graduates who want to learn the ropes.)

You'll find more sports-related volunteering positions in your local community. For example, if you want to teach tai chi, coach a peewee basketball class, or coordinate senior swimming, the best place to start is your local park district, YMCA, or Jewish Community Center. Organizations like these are usually happy to expand their offerings, but limited funding sometimes keeps them from hiring more staff.

ASK THE EXPERTS

My daughter has begun playing softball. I'd love to help but don't know the first thing about the sport.

There are plenty of things you can do. Consider helping out with fund-raising to help defray the costs for uniforms and equipment. Or you can also lend a hand by fitting kids with uniforms, supplying oranges at halftime, or taking on simple administrative tasks like keeping score.

I'd like to become a volunteer coach. Is there any training for that?

Yes, there is. Some school districts offer coaching clinics; call your school board or PTO and ask if they have one. If not, consider taking classes in the sport at your local YMCA, YWCA, or YMHA. Coaching camps, which are usually held in the summer, are another option. To find out more about them, contact the sport's official organization, for example, the U.S. Field Hockey Federation.

I'm interested in combining my love of sports with my wish to help the disabled. What can I do?

Organizations like Wheelchair Sports USA, the U.S. Association of Blind Athletes, and Special Olympics International all rely on volunteers for a myriad of positions. From coaching to keeping score, volunteers help provide a recreational outlet for disabled participants. You can find several links for sports organizations for the disabled from the U.S. Olympic Committee's Web site (**www.olympic-usa.org**). In the "Sports and News" box at the upper right, choose "Winter Paralympic Sports" or "Summer Paralympic Sports."

now what do I do?
Answers to common questions

I'd like to try my hand at teaching, but I am not ready to sign on as a professional teacher yet. What can I do to move toward that goal?

If you're interested in teaching, why not join AmeriCorps? A large portion of AmeriCorps opportunities involve setting up tutoring programs, training tutors, and working with kids. In return for your time, you'll get a modest stipend and living allowance, and education awards that you can use to wipe out student loans or pay for school. Visit **www.americorps.org** or call the Corporation for National Community Service at 202-606-5000 for more information. Another organization that trains new teachers is Teach for America. Check out their Web site at **www.teachforamerica.org**.

What about volunteering for my alma mater?

Colleges and universities need your help too. The best place to start is your school's alumni association. A common way to help is with recruitment and retention: You can represent your alma mater at your local high school's college night, or get hooked up with a student who has applied. For example, a dentist might get paired up with a predental student to answer her questions or address her concerns the following year. Or you might get paired with a first-year student to touch base with him and help ensure he returns the following year. If you'd like to work directly for a particular department, say, architecture, contact that office directly. But if you find yourself struggling to connect with the right person, take a deep breath and call the alumni association—they can often help you find what you're looking for, even if it's not part of their official volunteer program.

After 45 years in the business world, I've decided to retire. Are there any ways that I can use my experience to help others?

Sure. Consider contacting your local high school or college to see if you can tutor students in business classes. For a more formal mentoring program, contact SCORE—the Service Corps of Retired Executives. They provide counseling and workshops to small business owners on a wide variety of business issues. Once you join, you'll go through a 90-day training program (the Counselor Professional Development Program) before you begin helping out. Visit **www.score.org** or call 800-634-0245.

I noticed that there are some children from Latin America who are new to my children's school, and I am worried about how they are fitting in. Is there anything I can do to help them?

Inquire about "diversity" initiatives at your school. A number of schools have diversity programs in place to help smooth the transition of foreign students.

Now where do I go?!

CONTACTS

USAFreedomCorps
www.usafreedomcorps.gov
The government's new comprehensive clearinghouse helps you find local volunteer opportunities.

City Cares
404-875-7334
www.citycares.org
Alliance of volunteer organizations.

National Mentoring Partnership
703-224-2200
www.mentoring.org
Information on mentoring programs, techniques, and improvement.

Girl Scouts and Brownies
800-478-7248
www.girlscouts.org

Boy Scouts and Cub Scouts
www.scouting.org

Big Brothers Big Sisters of America
215-567-7000
www.bbbsa.org

Boys and Girls Clubs of America
404-487-5700
www.bgca.org

America's Promise
www.americaspromise.org
Colin Powell's national program to build character in our nation's youth.

Young Audiences
212-831-8110
www.youngaudiences.org
Integrates the arts into education.

BOOKS

The Volunteer Tutor's Toolbox
By Beth Ann Herrmann

Stand by Me: The Risks and Rewards of Mentoring Today's Youth
By Jean E. Rhodes

Book Buddies
By Francine R. Johnston, Marcia Invernizzi, and Connie Juel

Help America Read: A Handbook for Volunteers
By Gay Su Pinnell, Irene C. Fountas, and Arene C. Fountas

Help! I'm a Volunteer Youth Worker
By Doug Fields

101 Things Parents Should Know Before Volunteering to Coach Their Kids' Sports Teams
By Gary S. Goodman

8

Arts and sciences

Helping out in libraries, museums, and other places of culture enhances our country's well-being.

why the arts and sciences matter

Onward and upward

When it comes to making people's lives better, volunteering for institutions devoted to the arts and sciences may not seem as "important" as working in a nursing home or a hospital. But supporting libraries, symphony orchestras, museums, botanical gardens, and similar institutions contributes to our country's overall well-being by ensuring the survival of these life-enhancing experiences.

Since most of these institutions and organizations charge user fees for their services, you might think that their costs are covered. Not so. For example, just to break even, a large symphony orchestra must raise an average of $42 per seat—and that's in addition to the proceeds from the ticket sale! The same is true for most types of organizations covered in this chapter. Not only do these groups need private donations to stay in business, they also desperately need volunteers.

Maybe you're concerned that cultural and scientific pursuits are just for the wealthy and highly educated. This too is a misconception. Average citizens benefit from local music festivals, reading hours for children at the local library, and special events held at museums. Some cultural organizations reach out and help brighten the day for homebound seniors, the infirm, disadvantaged youth, and other downtrodden folks, often traveling to nursing homes, hospitals, and family shelters to share their art, music, or books.

ASK THE EXPERTS

What is a docent?

Docent comes from the Latin word meaning "to teach." Common in museums, libraries, zoos, and aquariums, these special volunteers are committed to teaching visitors and helping bring the exhibitions and displays to life. A museum docent, for example, might lead a group of children on a tour through the North American Indian Hall, where they learn how early Native Americans lived. She then might lead an informal seminar, using props like antlers, deerskin pelts, moccasins, and arrow-heads while engaging the kids in dialogue. Note: Before they can start volunteering, docents have to go through in-depth training to familiarize themselves with the exhibits and learn to work with visitors.

Can volunteering for an arts group help me change jobs?

Sure. Many opportunities, like becoming a docent or working at the information desk, allow you to get intimately familiar with the organization you're helping. These visible positions also let you meet people in other departments. Once you've started volunteering—and people get to know you—it's easier to network and land a paid position in the department that fits.

TURNING POINT

My first grader was very upset with me because many of the other children's mommies were helping out at his school all the time, but I couldn't because of my job. Or so I thought. During a parent/teacher conference, I mentioned my plight to his teacher. She suggested that I volunteer to lead a one-time art activity. Did I have any ideas? I said my son and I loved to paint stones. So she urged me to do a rock-painting project. Sure enough, I took a morning off from work and brought in a box of stones and some paint and my son's favorite book about fossils, and the kids were thrilled. No one was happier than my son. It was such a success, in fact, that I plan to do it again soon. I learned that you don't have to be a full-time volunteer; little bits here and there help a lot too!

—Babs C., Bedford, New York

libraries

Work for bookworms

If you're a bookworm or an information junkie, your local library is a great place to volunteer. While specialized libraries (like law and business libraries) are generally staffed by professionals, public libraries and school libraries usually rely on volunteers to help keep things running smoothly.

Friends of the Library and other library support organizations are nonprofit membership organizations that help turn good libraries into great ones. These groups usually provide standard volunteer services, helping to organize ongoing programs like monthly book groups, author events, or providing Books on Wheels to shut-ins. They also help organize fund-raisers—often an annual book sale. Modest dues help cover their costs, and members can participate as much or as little as they want.

Libraries often have seasonal programs, and volunteers often help to set them up and run them. A summer reading program for kids, for example, might need help signing up participants and then greeting them when they arrive.

If you'd prefer to volunteer in a certain area, simply contact the manager of the appropriate department of the public library. If you're not sure what you'd like to do, ask if the library has a volunteer coordinator or a "friends" organization.

ASK THE EXPERTS

Do libraries need help working with groups of schoolchildren?

Like museums and zoos, libraries use volunteer docents to give tours to visiting groups, be they from schools or retirement homes. Training is provided, so no special skills are needed. The best docents are people who enjoy working with others and have a genuine love and appreciation for libraries. Remember, however, that if your volunteer work will be exclusively with children, a background check will probably be required.

Is there any behind-the-scenes work that's needed?

Most libraries have computer centers that need volunteers to show patrons how to use the Internet and the online catalog. Most also need help mending books (regluing, taping spines) and shelving books (which, with all the stooping and kneeling, can be a physical challenge). The nature of these opportunities often require volunteers to commit to a fixed number of hours per week for at least six months to a year.

museums

Most museums are private nonprofits that are not affiliated with the government, so they rely on local community support to operate. Because of perpetual budget squeezes, volunteers for everything from fund-raising drives to gift shop inventory and accounting are critical to operations.

A museum's volunteer needs will depend on its size. A small, local historical museum might need help with tasks as varied as washing the windows, taking tickets, and educating visitors. Larger institutions have more needs, and work with specialized clusters of volunteers. These might include:

- **Educational** Specially trained docents give tours to adults or to children.

- **Curatorial** Behind-the-scenes volunteers help full-time curators to preserve the museum's inventory— whether they're paintings or insect collections.

- **Cataloguing** Volunteers help tag, number, and date individual pieces.

- **Visitor Services** Volunteers greet the public, take tickets, and help out in the gift shop.

- **Community Outreach** Volunteers bring educational programs or collections to local schools, nursing homes, or community centers.

Training is provided for most of these positions, so a weekly commitment is often required. But you may enjoy perks like free or discounted admission, and tickets to popular exhibits.

ASK THE EXPERTS

How can I get started volunteering at a museum?

Your local Volunteer Centers, part of the Points of Light Foundations & Volunteer Center National Network, make it easy to find out what volunteer positions are available. Or contact the museum directly and ask for the volunteer coordinator. Many museums have Web sites that post volunteer positions, so going online is also a good way to see what kinds of exhibits and departments they have.

I'm looking for short-term volunteer opportunities. Do museums have any?

Yes. Many museums have temporary exhibits during the year that need volunteer help. When you don't want to commit to a regular volunteer schedule, or you find yourself with a fixed amount of time to spare (day, week, month), ask the museum if they need help setting up, running, or taking down a special event or exhibit.

Museums sound so, well, boring. Are they?

Not at all! You might be surprised at the interesting variety of museums that need help. Air and space museums focus on airplane history, flight history, and space travel. Art museums showcase not only paintings but decorative arts like ceramics, sculpture, and textiles. If you enjoy kids, check out your local children's museum, which is interactive and experience-based. Other types of museums include halls of fame (like the Pro Football Hall of Fame in Canton, Ohio), maritime museums (which focus on boats of every sort), natural history (focused on the study of rocks, plants, animals, ancient civilizations, and dinosaurs), and science and technology (with exhibits that make nature, space, or scientific principles like physics understandable for visitors).

performing arts

Behind the scenes

Organizations devoted to the performing arts—live theater, opera, symphony, ballet—always need a variety of help. Community theater, in fact, is nearly 100% volunteer-based. From the board of directors to the costume designers to the actors/dancers/musicians themselves, all are unpaid.

If you have technical skills to share, local theater is a good outlet. Electricians can help design and plan the lighting. Visual artists can pitch in with scenery. Carpenters can help build the stage. And if you have an eye for style, finding costumes in used-clothing stores can be fun. Performing arts organizations also need clerical and fund-raising help.

The most common volunteer position at the theater (and perhaps the easiest) is ushering. In return for showing up early, handing out programs, taking tickets, and showing patrons to their seats, you get to see the show for free. Just call the box office, which will put you in touch with the house manager.

Ask the Experts

I love ballroom dancing. Are there places where I could volunteer?

Yes indeed! The U.S. Ballroom Dance Association is an all-volunteer organization that has 150 local chapters with a variety of needs, including dancers. (Contact them at **www.usabda.org/home/index.cfm** or 800-447-9047). Because the aim of the organization is to promote ballroom dance, chapters need people from their community to give public dance demonstrations in malls, schools, and nursing homes. You can also volunteer to help with other needs.

I've always had a secret passion for the circus. Can I volunteer—without running away?

If you're a Shriner, you can volunteer for the Shriners Circus—selling tickets, working the concession stands, and marketing and promoting the shows that raise money for the Shriners children's hospitals. If you live in the Wisconsin area, the Circus World Museum needs volunteers to meet and greet bands that visit the museum, provide tours to visitors, and perform other duties. Call 608-356-8341 for more information. If you're a real circus fanatic, consider joining the Circus Fans Association of America (**www.circusfans.org**).

zoos and aquariums

Animal magnetism

If the wonderful world of wildlife is one of your primary interests, consider volunteering at a zoo or an aquarium. You could find yourself doing everything from cutting up veggies for the chimpanzees' breakfast to monitoring the water quality in the manatee tank. Volunteers can even enrich zoo animals' lives by making toys for them—for example, papier-mâché balls that tiger and bear cubs can bat around or wrestle with.

Basic volunteer positions—greeter, gift shop clerk, information booth attendant, and the like—are always needed at zoos and aquariums. Both also rely on docents to educate the public about animals or fish. You don't need special experience to be a docent—just a love of wildlife, nature, people, and a commitment to work a three-hour shift every other week. But before you're allowed to run wild, you'll need training. At one New Jersey zoo, for example, docents attend 10 four-hour classes over the course of 10 weeks before giving their first tour. Docents are often given some on-the-job training as well.

Some zoos and aquariums are supported by "friends" organizations, which provide a pool of volunteers. Either contact a zoo or aquarium directly (asking for the volunteer coordinator), or check out their Web sites—many zoos and aquariums post volunteer opportunities online. Not only can the work be fun, but you may be able to enjoy perks like free admission, discounts at shops and restaurants, and free (or discounted) classes, parking, and newsletters.

ASK THE EXPERTS

I've done extensive deep-sea diving. Are there any aquariums that might need my help?

Yes. Aquariums look for divers to help the staff with their "cleaning dives," which ensure that the tank environment is as clean as possible.

I'm a frustrated high-rise dweller itching to get my hands dirty. Is there any way to combine my love for animals with my green thumb?

Maybe. Some zoos need gardeners to help the staff horticulturists with their gardening. If you like digging, tilling, watering, weeding, planting, pruning, mulching, and raking, this could be for you.

Can I volunteer for a short-term commitment at an aquarium or zoo?

Possibly. To find out, call your local zoo or aquarium to see if they have special events you can help with. Special events—usually centered around holidays or festivals—are a great way to meet people or to volunteer with your family, friends, or coworkers. For example, "Boo Zoo" volunteers might hand out candy to trick-or-treating tots, pose as a monster, or help decorate the haunted house.

botanical gardens, arboretums, conservatories

Green thoughts in a green shade

Botanical gardens and arboretums are involved with plant conservation, ecological restoration work, and contributing to the health and well-being of the environment. And because they're usually nonprofit organizations, volunteers are always needed.

A botanical garden is a public garden where almost any type of plant is grown, including trees, shrubs, and flowers. An arboretum, meanwhile, is a type of botanical garden that grows only trees and shrubs. Conservatories, which are generally a part of a botanical garden or arboretum, are the glass buildings that some plants are grown in.

These institutions are museums of a sort—with living collections. And like museums, they need volunteers to educate the public, keep track of and label their collections, and work in the gift shop and cafeteria. The larger institutions have libraries that might even need help.

To get involved, contact your local botanical garden or arboretum and ask for the volunteer coordinator. If you're not sure where to start, contact the American Association of Botanical Gardens and Arboreta Web site (**www.aabga.org**).

ASK THE EXPERTS

Are there any short-term or seasonal opportunities at botanical gardens?

Sure! You can help with the special exhibits (like the chrysanthemum show) by checking tickets or by being stationed along the paths to answer questions. Or assist with the annual plant sale by helping to set up or staff the sales table or cashier lines. Or sell tickets to the Garden Art Festival.

To be honest, I was hoping for something a little more hands-on than working in the gift shop. What type of direct opportunities are there?

If you want to get your hands dirty, there are ample opportunities at botanical gardens and arboretums to help with weeding, planting, pruning, sowing seeds, transplanting, staking and trimming plants, and washing pots. Or if you prefer a not-so-dirty job, you can help maintain collections and plant records by doing research, entering data, and mapping the display gardens, or you might monitor rare plants in the local area.

history and genealogy

Like other museums, historical museums and societies need help giving tours to visitors or working in hands-on galleries. A volunteer stationed in a house restored to its pre–Civil War splendor might be expected to relate the history of the house to visitors and talk about its furnishings and former inhabitants.

Some historical society volunteers greet visiting school groups, and others might work in its research center helping visitors find what they're looking for. No experience? No problem—depending on your position, you'll get training on touring techniques and the content of the exhibit or organization that you'll be explaining.

Another kind of history endeavor for which you can volunteer is more intangible: genealogy, the tracing of ancestry. Volunteerism is also essential to the genealogy process. Many Internet sites encourage volunteers to help others, especially after they've been helped by someone else. For example, Random Acts of Genealogical Kindness (**www. raogk.org**) asks its volunteers to help family-tree seekers by videotaping local cemeteries or visiting county courthouses or archives at least once a month. At **www.genealogy today.com** you can volunteer to be part of "Team Roots" to answer visitors' questions ("What's a third cousin?" or "How do I find out what my last name means?") or to help manage the site itself. You can also list your last name and be a resource for others with the same last name. Or peruse the "Lost and Found" database to help people track down information on a specific ancestor.

ASK THE EXPERTS

Our local historical society usually requires a one-year commitment to volunteer. Do you think there might be any one-time opportunities to volunteer to see if I like it—before I commit?

Sure. Ask if you can help with their annual fund-raiser or other special event. Most nonprofits need periodic help with everything from finding sponsors to hanging posters to taking tickets at the door.

I'm a genealogy buff. How else can I help people with their search?

If you live near a cemetery, you can pitch in by recording the information from tombstones in old graveyards. (To learn more, visit **www.cemeteryjunction.com**). Or, if you own genealogical research books and want to share information, visit Books We Own (**www.rootsweb.com/~bwo**). You can post your resources and offer to look up genealogical information, after which you either e-mail or snail-mail it to others who request it.

I'd like to help people with their genealogy hunt but prefer to do it in person. Where can I do that?

Check out your local historical societies, which house microfilm of old newspapers, old phone books and maps, and other resources from your city. Once you've gone through training, you'll be able to help local visitors dig up their family roots.

now what do I do?
Answers to common questions

I'm an attorney and enjoy the arts. Is there any way to volunteer legal services to cultural organizations?

You bet. There are many "Volunteer Lawyers for the Arts" organizations throughout the country. For example Volunteer Lawyers for the Arts (New York), Philadelphia Volunteer Lawyers for the Arts, St. Louis Volunteer Lawyers and Accountants for the Arts, and California Lawyers for the Arts all provide avenues for attorneys to provide pro bono (free) legal services, like negotiating a ballet dancer's contract, incorporating a new dance troupe, or negotiating a lease for an art gallery. If you can't find your nearest organization, check out the National Endowment for the Arts at **www.arts.gov/artforms/Manage/VLA2.html** for a list of these organizations.

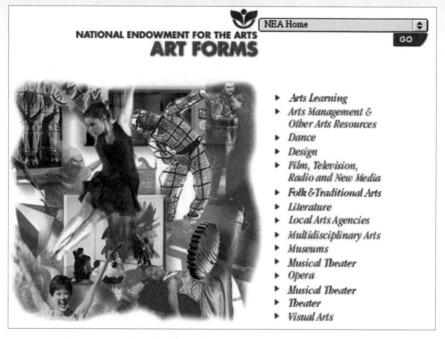

I want to give my time but don't really know anything about flowers, the theater, or culture. How can I start?

If you're ready to dive in and make a commitment, most of these organizations need help in their gift shops and cafeterias. And if you really want to learn about them, offer to work the information desk at the zoo, library, museum, or historical society. Once you've gone through training and have worked for a while, you'll know more than the employees do!

I want to be an actor. Can volunteering in the arts help?

Sure. Volunteering to help with local theater productions is a great way to make connections in the acting world. And if you ace your audition, landing even a minor role will beef up your resumé. Volunteer as an usher or work behind the scenes on lighting, costumes, building sets, or other tasks until you get the acting roles you want.

I really want to volunteer to work with animals, but I don't have any experience. Can I still volunteer?

Large organizations like zoos and aquariums have the resources to train volunteers to work with animals. If there are no zoos or aquariums nearby, consider smaller organizations like a local ASPCA chapter. They can't afford to officially train volunteers, but they can always use volunteer help—and you'll pick up some of the necessary skills as you work.

Now where do I go?!

CONTACTS

www.zoos-worldwide.com
Find a zoo or aquarium anywhere in the world.

www.azadocents.org
Association of Zoo & Aquarium Docents

American Association of Botanical Gardens and Arboreta
www.aabga.org

Geneaology Today
www.geneaologytoday.com

City Cares
404-875-7334
www.citycares.org

BOOKS

Volunteering to Help with Animals
By Claudia Isler

Museum Volunteers: Good Practice in the Management of Volunteers
By Sinclair Goodlad and Stephanie McIvor

Volunteers in Libraries
By Rashelle S. Karp

9

Environmental opportunities

No experience is necessary,
just a desire to help protect
our natural resources.

concern for the environment

Through human use and misuse, the country's natural resources are eroding. Litter and chemicals pollute rivers and streams, and many wildlife species are disappearing. Yet the demand for use of our resources continues to skyrocket.

Volunteer opportunities abound in the independent or nonprofit organizations whose goal is to influence public awareness of—and public policy on—the environment. But where do you turn when you're ready to get your hands dirty to clean up the land and water? Surprisingly, most of these volunteer opportunities can be found through the government, which has the greatest need.

Think about it—who owns the vast majority of this country's land, forests, parks, and rivers? Uncle Sam does, and he wants YOU to help keep them clean. To make it easy for potential volunteers to sign up, the federal government has created **www.volunteer.gov/gov**, which is a portal to natural resource volunteer opportunities throughout the country. You can also work to improve the environment through state and local governments and organizations.

Green Thumbs, Red Tape

The country's environment and natural resources are watched over by a vast federal bureaucracy. Environmental volunteers and groups work within this context, supporting the federal authorities.

The Department of the Interior

Bureau of Land Management (BLM)
helps preserve and maintain public lands.

U.S. Geological Survey (USGS)
provides scientific information to increase understanding of the earth so that it can be better managed.

National Parks Service (NPS)
promotes the conservation of our national parks' scenery and wildlife.

U.S. Fish & Wildlife Service (FWS)
conserves America's plants, animals, and fish, and their habitats.

The U.S. Department of Agriculture (USDA)

National Resources Conservation Center (NRCS)
works with private landowners (farmers and ranchers) to encourage them to conserve and improve the environment.

Forest Service (FS)
protects the public forests.

Other Agencies

Army Corps of Engineers
oversees some 12 million acres of land and water for both recreation and natural resource purposes.

maintaining the land

Your country needs you—literally

The U.S. Bureau of Land Management cares for 264 million acres of land, including campsites, nature centers, recreation areas, and vast areas that aren't developed at all. Currently, more than 20,000 volunteers a year contribute to maintaining this overwhelming amount of land, whether mapping it, or simply picking up trash from prairies and trails. To volunteer, check your local phone book in the blue pages under Department of Interior, Bureau of Land Management. You can also visit **www.blm.gov/** for more information about the Bureau, or **www.volunteer.gov/gov** for volunteer opportunities.

Many Earth Team volunteers work directly with farmers to help conserve the land.

At the same time, more than 40,000 people per year serve the National Resources Conservation Service's Earth Team. These volunteers work directly with conservation professionals to encourage farmers, ranchers, and other private landowners to conserve and improve the environment. The team finds land that's in danger of erosion, then teaches owners how to protect it. Volunteers can also work in schools teaching conservation. No experience is necessary—just a desire to help the environment. To work with the Earth Team, call 888-526-3227 or **www.nrcs.usda.gov** to locate your state volunteer coordinator.

ASK THE EXPERTS

Is there any way I can combine land cleanup with my passion for hiking?

The American Discovery Trail (ADT) (**www.discoverytrail.org**) is a string of local trails (including pioneer trails) that have been connected to create a 6,300-mile coast-to-coast trail. Stretching from California to Delaware, the ADT weaves through 14 national parks, 16 national forests, and a number of big cities. Volunteers are needed to help build sections of the trail, pick up trash, and clear away brush, and the work shifts are overseen by local organizations. Call 800-663-2387 to request a volunteer packet, to be referred to a local trail club, or to locate your state's ADT Coordinator. On National Trails Day (first Saturday in June), local hiking organizations create their own programs, which might include trail building and maintenance. For more information or to find a local organization, contact the American Hiking Society at 301-565-6704 or **www.american hiking.org**.

Can I volunteer to do cleanup alongside my friends or family?

There are a several countrywide opportunities where you can work shoulder to shoulder with other volunteers. The excitement generated by having so many volunteers—and seeing the fruits of your labor—re-energizes volunteers and environmental employees alike. One opportunity comes on National Public Lands Day (**www.npld.com**), which takes place on the last Saturday of September.

preserving parks and forests

The voice of experience

The National Park Service (NPS) uses more than 120,000 volunteers a year—from every state and nearly every country in the world—to help maintain hundreds of U.S. national parks, recreation areas, monuments, and historical sites. In 1970, the service's Volunteers-In-Parks Program (VIP) was established by law to create a way for people to help preserve and protect our natural and cultural heritage for future generations.

Park volunteer opportunities range from the ordinary (cleaning trash from the beaches) to the exotic (serving as a lighthouse tour guide in the Florida Keys to provide visitors with cultural, historical, and environmental information). Maybe you'd like to take a few weeks off in the summer and visit historic parts of the country that you've never seen. The Florida Everglades needs volunteers to collect water and plant-life data. The Grand Canyon staff needs help planting seedlings, pulling weeds, and collecting seeds on the South Rim. These kinds of activities can last anywhere from one day to one month.

To find out more about the parks, visit **www.nps.gov** or check the blue pages in your phone book under Department of Interior, National Park Service. When you're ready to search for volunteer opportunities, click on **www.volunteer.gov/gov**.

ASK THE EXPERTS

What is the Army Corps of Engineers?

The U.S. Army Corps of Engineers (**www.usace.army.mil**) is the military's public-works division. Established in 1775, the USACE originally helped build fortifications near Boston at Bunker Hill. Today it provides engineering services to the nation for any project centered on the country's rivers and lakes. Volunteer jobs include acting as campground hosts on lakefront parks, as visitors center docents, and as information desk volunteers. Call their Volunteer Clearinghouse at 800-865-8337 or visit **www.volunteer.gov/gov**. They'll hook you up with any project in the country that interests you and mail information about various opportunities.

What's a campground host?

Campground hosts usually work 20 hours a week—greeting visitors, answering questions, collecting fees, or performing minor cleaning and maintenance. In exchange, they're often given a free campsite and utilities hookups. Hosts are needed for the National Parks, National Forests, and the USACE.

Do the national forests offer similar opportunities?

The nearly 200 national forests and national grasslands have similar needs. People act as campground hosts, plant seeds or trees in damaged areas, build or repair fences and picnic tables, work in ranger stations to greet visitors, and answer phones and reply to mail. Visit **www.fs.fed.us** or check the blue pages under U.S. Government Department of Agriculture, Forest Service, to find the forest near you, or **www.volunteer.gov/gov** for specific opportunities.

helping animals

Endearing and endangered

The U.S. Fish and Wildlife Service (**www.fws.gov**) focuses on conserving fish and marine mammals, wildlife, and plants. Most volunteer opportunities involve helping preserve habitats rather than working directly with animals—although some include animal contact. The goal is to keep animals off the endangered species lists and to keep their population levels healthy.

Some volunteers count butterflies to see if the population is increasing or decreasing. Others pick up and analyze droppings to make sure birds are eating their natural food sources. Another opportunity is to act as a docent in a wildlife refuge visitors center, answering visitors' questions and leading discussions. Or you could be a Songbird Nest Box Monitor—from April through August, volunteers monitor several nest boxes once a week to check for nests, eggs, and fledglings.

If you want to join the more than 36,000 FWS volunteers, apply online at **www.volunteer.gov/gov**, e-mail volunteers@fws.gov, or check the blue pages in your phone book under U.S. Government, Department of the Interior, Fish and Wildlife Service, for the nearest regional office, refuge, or fish hatchery.

Monitor the lives of frogs and toads as a volunteer for Frogwatch USA.

ASK THE EXPERTS

I'm a little nervous about making an ongoing volunteer commitment, but I still would like to help protect the environment. Can I?

Yes. If you want to dip your toe (or even your entire leg) in the water, consider being an Atlantic Salmon Fry Stocker. Each spring, hundreds of volunteers walk through streams in the states of Connecticut, Massachusetts, and Vermont to "stock baby salmon." This helps restore Atlantic Salmon to the Connecticut River. Volunteer training—and waders—are provided. Contact the U.S. Fish and Wildlife Service or check out their Web site: **www.fws.gov**.

I'm a frog fanatic. How can I help them?

In neighborhoods across the nation, Frogwatch USA volunteers collect information about frog and toad populations. Contact the Frogwatch USA Coordinator, Patuxent Wildlife Research Center, U.S. Geological Survey—Biological Resources Division, at 301-497-5840 or click to **www.mp2-pwrc.usgs.gov/frogwatch** or e-mail frogwatch@nfw.gov.

rivers and waters

Blue-green treasures

Oceans, lakes, and rivers are all home to delicate ecosystems and wildlife, which need protection and preservation.

The Ocean Conservancy is a national nonprofit organization whose Annual International Coastal Cleanup (third Saturday of September) rounds up volunteers from all over the country—and the world—to remove trash from the shores of our rivers, lakes, and oceans.

Volunteers also collect data about this debris, which reduces future marine debris. For example, the most common item is cigarette butts. Many people are unaware that filters are made of nonbiodegradable plastic, which is harmful to all living things.

If you're looking to make a difference a little closer to home, the U.S. Fish and Wildlife Service's Adopt-a-Boat-Landing will put you in charge of cleaning up litter and debris from an assigned boat landing twice a year. You'll also be responsible for telling the district office if any repairs or maintenance are needed.

Combine your love of the outdoors with your clean streak as a volunteer for the Ocean Conservancy, top. Volunteers also gather data on debris and water quality, right.

ASK THE EXPERTS

I'm concerned about the quality of the water in rivers and lakes. Is there anything I can do to help?

Yes—by monitoring water. Whether water is polluted or used for drinking or swimming, volunteers are needed to help monitor water sources by analyzing water samples. They evaluate water habitats for plants and animals, and can also collect and track beach debris. To get involved with water monitoring, check out the Environmental Protection Agency's water monitoring program (**www.epa.gov/owow/monitoring/volunteer**).

How can I get started?

Get involved by contacting the U.S. Fish and Wildlife Service through **www.volunteer.gov/gov** or the Ocean Conservancy at 202-429-5609 or **www.ocean conservancy.org**.

TURNING POINT

I was heartbroken after my relationship ended, so I decided to volunteer to distract myself from the blues. Since I love visiting the stream that runs through my town, I joined the EPA's volunteer water monitoring program. (I knew that being "forced" to go there would lift my spirits.) Not only did I enjoy helping monitor and clean up the local water, but I also met my fiancé!

—Linda T., Cove Springs, Oregon

local beautification

Sprucing up your community

In most cases, the volunteer opportunities for lands, parks, forests, and water will help beautify your local community. But a few additional opportunities exist for helping to spruce up your neighborhood.

Contact your local park district's volunteer coordinator to find out about local beautification or recycling volunteer needs. You can also pitch in with your community's beautification through your local civic groups, including the chamber of commerce, garden club, or other groups.

Some of these groups are connected with the group Keep America Beautiful (KAB), a national organization that enables individuals and community organizations to beautify their communities by providing them with tools, training, and resources. Each of the 500 community affiliates and 28 state affiliates has a different focus, and efforts range from beautification to litter control to environmental education in the schools. Some affiliates are actually part of the state or local government.

By contacting KAB you can join your local affiliate—or start your own—so you can paint park benches, pull weeds, teach children about the environment, or clean up lakefront litter. Call 203-323-8987 or click to **www.kab.org**.

ASK THE EXPERTS

How can I help with litter along our roads and highways?

Many schools, nonprofits, and businesses take part in Adopt A Highway (**www.adoptahighway.com**), a program that cleans up a designated stretch of road on the group's behalf, in exchange for a sponsorship fee. If your group wants to do the work itself, work with your local department of transportation to identify the particular street and work out the details.

Are there any one-time opportunities for cleanup?

One-time opportunities are virtually unlimited each spring, during the Great American Cleanup, the largest community beautification program in the U.S. Thousands of communities plant trees and flowers, clean up parks and shorelines, and collect recyclables. Checking the Keep America Beautiful Web site (**www.kab.org**) will let you know whether your community participates. If it doesn't, the site will give you the name of your state leader (with contact information) and instructions for starting your own local Great American Cleanup program.

I can't find a local beautification program. What can I do?

Start one! If your community organization needs helping getting a local cleanup or beautification program off the ground, the National Center for Recreation and Conservation (**www.ncrc.nps.gov**) can help. A division of the National Park Service, the NCRC helps citizen groups enhance their local parks, trails, and rivers as a "junior partner" of local groups.

now what do I do?
Answers to common questions

My mother suggested I join the local garden club if I want to help the environment. What opportunities can I find there?

Garden clubs take their civic and environmental responsibilities very seriously and are often very involved in helping the environment. Members may volunteer to tend the herb garden in the local park or the rose garden on the street corner, decorate the public library for Christmas, or provide garden therapy for seniors at the retirement home To find a garden club near you check out **www.gardenclub.org**.

What about 4-H programs?

The 4-H clubs took root about 100 years ago, when educators began to focus on young people's needs and introduced nature study to enhance agricultural education. The clubs, common in rural areas and often con-nected with colleges and universities, have over 600,000 volunteers—but still need your help. If you have a special interest in the environment (or other skills like photography, computers, or public speaking), see if you can arrange to teach the subject to club members. To find your nearest club, visit **www.4-h.org/fourhweb/statelist.shtml** or contact your county's Cooperative Extension office.

What about organizations like the Sierra Club and Greenpeace?

If you enjoy hiking or backpacking, Sierra Club outings provide you with ways to combine your favorite leisure activities with social interaction—and environmental cleanup. To learn more, visit **www.sierraclub.org**. Common service trips include helping the Forest Service or Park Service to maintain trails, clean up trash and campsites, and remove nonnative plants from a site. Greenpeace (**www.greenpeace.org**) focuses on advocacy (see page 34–35). If you join this activist network, you can help promote environmen-tal causes by writing letters or joining peaceful demonstrations

I'd like to take a few months off work to volunteer in an exotic area, but I'm not comfortable traveling abroad. Any suggestions?

Contact the Earthwatch Institute (**www.earthwatch.org**). This is an organization that promotes conservation of the earth's natural resources through partnerships among scientists, the general public, teachers, and businesses. You can help monitor Hawaii's active volcanoes and offer other research assistance, like collecting and analyzing data and working with volcano and earthquake monitoring equipment. If you're willing to work full time for at least three months, housing is provided. You'll find information at **http://hvo.wr.usgs.gov/volunteer**.

I'd like to volunteer in the recycling area. What can I do?

Most towns are active in recycling, but their volunteer programs differ—so start by calling your city hall's public works or environmental services department. Block leader programs, based on a wildly successful program in Boulder, Colorado, designate residents of each block to serve as recycling advocates. The local "answer man," a block leader, keeps neighbors up to date on recycling methods. Noncivic programs are operated as well. Local schools and Boy Scout and Girl Scout troops often organize recycling drives to raise funds—and they can always use some extra help. Your local Keep America Beautiful affiliate can also point you in the right direction for recycling volunteering.

Now where do I go?!

CONTACTS

Volunteer.Gov/Gov
www.volunteer.gov/gov
The government's comprehensive site to find natural resource volunteering opportunities.

Earth Share
800-875-3863
www.earthshare.org
Alliance of environmental groups that promotes donations through workplace payroll deductions.

Earth Systems
www.earthsystems.org/ways/
Making a difference in the lives of the homeless.

Youth Corps for Animals
www.youthforanimals.org/
Helps young people find animal-related volunteer opportunities.

Nature Conservancy
800-628-6860
www.nature.org
Works with communities, businesses, and individuals to protect the environment.

BOOKS

Volunteering to Help the Environment
By Suzanne J. Murdico

Volunteer Vacations: Short-Term Adventures That Will Benefit You and Others
By Bill McMillon and Edward Asner

10

Global issues

It's about living—and helping—
in another culture.

volunteering abroad

Be sure you can
go the distance

If you're looking for a challenge, consider volunteering abroad. A stint overseas can be a life-changing experience. Maybe you want to paint a Mexican orphanage for a week, mentor Bolivian street kids for a few months, or teach English in China. These are just a few of the actual short-term programs you'll find by searching **www.volunteerabroad.com**. Joining the Peace Corps, (**www.peacecorps.org**), on the other hand, requires a minimum commitment of two years plus training. In either case, volunteering abroad calls for a little soul-searching before you go.

What's your priority—location or skill? Some people are itching to visit a particular part of the world and will pitch in with whatever work needs to be done there. Other folks, like doctors and nurses, don't really care where their skills will be applied.

What's your motivation? If you're only looking for a cheap vacation, don't do it. Also, check your expectations about the impact you will make. If you have a romantic vision about solving world hunger or other developing-nation problems, you'll be disappointed. The most successful overseas volunteers show up ready to serve in any capacity.

Who's the sponsoring organization? Is it governmental, nonprofit, or for-profit? If it's a for-profit organization, how much money do they contribute to the community? Are they faith-based or secular? It's important that your values are compatible with those of the sponsoring organization.

What type of environment are you looking for? Can you handle rustic living conditions, or do you need more comfortable accommodations? Do you already speak another language fluently? Are you looking to learn or improve your knowledge of another language? Or would you feel most comfortable if no foreign language skills are required?

What's your budget? While some projects provide travel and accommodations, most don't. You might be responsible for your airfare, the cost of room and board, and a program fee. If money is a problem, however, don't give up on joining. Many groups provide guidance on how to make it possible.

What are your expectations? If you think you'll be hailed a hero, think again. Get ready to listen—and to learn—as you contribute to bettering a community's conditions. And remember, it's not just about laying bricks or teaching English. It's about life in another culture, so be respectful and polite.

ASK THE EXPERTS

How long should I expect to be gone?

International volunteer opportunities range from a week to several years. Most of the shorter-term opportunities are project-oriented, such as helping to build a rural school or helping doctors teach AIDS awareness in Africa. Longer-term projects, including the Peace Corps, require you to immerse yourself in the culture and become a visible member of the community.

How do I apply to join the Peace Corps?

As long as you have a college degree, are a U.S. citizen, and have some type of community service experience, your chances of being accepted are pretty good. Just make sure you've done your homework before you apply. After you've researched its Web site and understand the commitment, your local recruiter will send you an application. Be patient: The process of applying, interviewing, doing reference, legal, medical, and dental checks, and placement can take anywhere from five months to a year.

community development

Building for the future

If you're not sure where to begin, consider a community development program to improve general health and living conditions in underdeveloped areas. Even if you're unskilled, you can participate in building a school, clinic, or local hospital. Other projects, like setting up water-treatment facilities, planting trees, and simply cleaning up the streets are also available.

If you're part of a building or construction team, be prepared to sweat. Such work often requires intense physical labor for several hours a day. Make sure you find out what's expected of you—and that you're comfortable with it—before you sign up.

Also, expect very few of the amenities you're used to. You might be working to install a water pipeline for a small village with no infrastructure, electricity, or medical facilities. While less intense opportunities are available (like building, painting, and decorating playground facilities for preschool kids), you should still be prepared for long days and less-than-ideal facilities.

ASK THE EXPERTS

What sort of short-term community development opportunities are there?

Habitat for Humanity, which works both in the U.S. and abroad (**www.habitat.org**), has short-term Global Village trips (one to three weeks) that allow you to help build affordable housing for the needy. Volunteers team up with local community members to build bridges between cultures as well as decent homes for the poor.

Are there any ways I could help make volatile regions more peaceful?

Yes. Global Volunteers (**www.globalvolunteers.org** or 800-487-1074) sends people to the Glencree Centre for Reconciliation. Located in the Wicklow Mountains just south of Dublin, Glencree is a private Irish nonprofit dedicated to building peace by bringing citizens from Northern Ireland and the Republic of Ireland together in intensive workshops. Through direct dialogue, people with differing viewpoints are able to reach a higher level of understanding. Volunteers are needed to help with such routine maintenance as landscaping, painting, cleaning, and preparing meeting rooms.

My local church organizes an annual trip to a Venezuelan orphanage. I'd like to help, but I'm not a member. Would they mind if I tagged along?

It depends. Many churches or other religious organizations that provide their members with opportunities to volunteer abroad welcome people without regard to their religious beliefs or practices. Others require that everyone share a common faith. Why? The trip may be organized secondarily to knit the congregation closer together, and allowing nonmembers would defeat this purpose. Also, there may be prayer, worship, and other activities that you might not feel comfortable participating in. To find out if you are eligible, simply call the group's organizers and ask.

schools and education

Knowledge is power

While education is a constitutional right in the United States, this is not the case in many countries around the world. If you want to do your part to educate people who might otherwise go without instruction, consider teaching abroad. Opportunities abound, and include teaching English to Korean dockworkers, science to Rwandan children, or math to migrant farm children in Mexico. Or you could teach those who need instruction in health awareness or business skills. You could even teach other teachers, so that your work continues after you're gone.

Your students might be preschoolers or teens, or they might be adults seeking to improve their English and literacy skills so they can advance their careers and help the local economy. You might also seek out a specialized population—say, deaf children in Guadalajara, single women in China, or orphans in Mongolia. Among the groups who need volunteer teachers are Cross Cultural Solutions (**www.crossculturalsolutions.org** or 800-380-4777) and Global Service Corps (**www.globalservicecorps.org** or 415-788-3666 x128).

Don't be surprised if you're suddenly asked to help paint your classroom or help with other light maintenance work. Sometimes that's just part of the deal.

Teaching in Ghana is one of the many international volunteer opportunities offered by Cross Cultural Solutions.

ASK THE EXPERTS

As a volunteer teacher, do I have to commit long-term?

No. There are education programs that use volunteers for as little as two to four weeks. You can teach a short-term class, provide topical lectures, or simply help full-time teachers with their classes. Contact Volunteers for Peace (**www.vfp.org**) or Cross Cultural Solutions (**www.crossculturalsolutions.org** or 800-380-4777).

Do I have to be a certified teacher to volunteer?

Not usually. Many teaching and educational positions require only knowledge of the subject matter and a heart for helping others.

TURNING POINT

After graduating from college, I decided to join the Peace Corps and teach English in Guatemala for two years before starting my own teaching career. Unfortunately, a month before I left, I met the man of my dreams, and I was devastated that I would have to be apart from him. My first few months away were miserable. I missed Mike, the food was horrible, the bugs were terrible, and even though I was fairly fluent in Spanish, I missed speaking English. In fact, I missed just about everything about the United States. But after a few months of really understanding the conditions my students lived in, my perspective began to change. How could I lament the loss of pizza when some kids barely had enough to eat? Gratitude for my life back home began to sink in, I stopped sweating the small stuff, and I felt happy and fulfilled for the rest of my experience.

—Rita S., Tucson, Arizona

wildlife and conservation

All creatures great and small

If you have a strong interest in the environment and endangered plant and animal species, you can do your part to protect them. You can plant trees in Costa Rica, for example, or tag turtles on the beaches of the Galapagos, build a pond for dragonflies in Japan, or clear a trail in Belize's National Forest.

If you're determined to do environmental work abroad but aren't ready to get your hands dirty, work at the organizational level. This could mean helping to prevent water-supply contamination, designing projects to control erosion, or teaching farming techniques to farmers. Earthwatch (**www.earthwatch.org** or 800-776-0188) and Global Volunteers (**www.globalvolunteers.org** or 800-487-1074) both offer these opportunities. Or search **www.volunteerabroad.com** or **www.volunteerinternational.org** to learn of environmental opportunities.

Remember that you're fighting a hard battle against unhealthy habits, aggressive industrial expansion, and government indifference. So expect hard work!

ASK THE EXPERTS

What types of tasks might I be expected to do on an international environment expedition?

It could vary greatly—anything from counting fish on a coral reef to recording monkey mating rituals to helping scientists identify and count rare orchids or palm trees. Of course, there are more labor-intensive programs too, like helping to renovate an irrigation canal or a water-drainage ditch. If you're concerned, make sure to ask plenty of questions before you sign up.

It seems that most international volunteer programs are at least two weeks long. Aren't there any shorter ones?

Ironically, most overseas volunteers find that the time abroad goes too quickly. But if time constraints allow you to serve only for a short week or weekend, contact Earthwatch's Discovery Weekend Series (**www.earthwatch.org/discovery/allprojects.html**). Although these programs—offered in Europe, Japan, and Australia—last for only three to seven days, you'll still be able to participate in scientific investigations and enjoy a rewarding experience.

health and hygiene

More than just medicine

One of the most important ways to make a long-term impact overseas is in the area of healthcare. Over 90% of the 36 million people living with HIV/AIDS reside in developing countries and are desperate for education, treatment, and care. Epidemics, civil war, natural disasters, and poverty deny most residents of these countries the most basic healthcare needs.

If you're not a doctor or nurse, don't worry. There are plenty of support and educational opportunities. You can teach classes in basic hygiene or AIDS prevention, work in a lab testing for diabetes, or simply transport patients to receive medical care. If you help to build a hospital or help local leaders design basic sanitation systems or health programs, the fruits of your volunteer labors will remain long after you're gone.

Who knows? You might even get a hands-on experience. With a little training, you might be able to give hepatitis vaccinations to children in Gabon or basic eye exams to needy families in Bangladesh. Volunteer Optometric Service to Humanity (**www.vosh.org**) sends volunteers who are interested in providing basic eye care to underdeveloped countries—and you don't have to be an optometrist to take part.

If you're a doctor or nurse, be prepared to be creative, patient, and flexible. Opportunities to serve the millions of people who lack basic medical care are plentiful. Whether you're a practicing family doctor or a retired neurologist, your basic knowledge should be enough to help these individuals. Traditional resources are scarce, however, so you might end up boiling needles, dispensing basic penicillin instead of more sophisticated antibiotics, and washing and reusing plastic gloves.

Dr. Pamela Grim volunteers for Doctors of the World-USA, an international relief organization. For over 10 years Doctors of the World-USA has been saving lives in the Balkans.

Don't let yourself be limited to the normal definitions of healthcare—it doesn't have to be one-on-one. In Nicaragua, one dentist treated patients in 24 rural villages and trained nurses in a regional dental clinic. And in Belize, a clinical psychologist helped train the staff of a shelter for abused children.

A SK THE EXPERTS

If there are so few medical resources available in developing countries, how will volunteering really help?

While resources (including needles, basic medicines, and X rays) are generally inadequate, just feeling respected and cared for by another human being can make a big difference in these people's lives. Also, by educating people in basic hygiene issues (moving the latrine area away from the food tent, for example), future disease can be prevented.

I'm a doctor. Where can I find out more about medical positions?

To explore the medical positions available to volunteers, see the resources on page 193 or check out Health Volunteers Overseas (**www.hvousa.org**), International Medical Volunteers Association (**www.imva.org**), Doctors without Borders (**www.doc torswithoutborders.org**), or Doctors of the World (888-817-4357, **www.doctorsoftheworld.org**).

Dr. Victoria Sharp, (center) Chair of Board of Directors for Doctors of the World-USA, in Thailand along the Thai-Burma Border, where the organization is working to improve healthcare for Burmese migrants.

refugees and orphans

Adults and children from war-torn regions

Wars, famine, and disease don't just kill people. They uproot communities, break apart families, and send survivors fleeing. For example, over 14 million refugees have fled their homes worldwide, with over half from the Middle East and Africa. In Kenya, 245,000 people live in refugee camps.

Volunteers from the Lions Club distribute life-sustaining grain in Kenya during a famine.

Volunteers at these types of shelters help provide practical needs (for example, distributing food and clothing or repairing tents), emotional needs (providing friendship, encouragement, and hope for the future), and medical needs. In developing nations, volunteers are sometimes needed to help teach people the routine acts of daily living, like brushing their teeth and hair.

Children, whether they live in war-ravaged areas or not, are least able to make choices to change their situation. Many end up in orphanages. While some of these children are actually orphaned or unwanted, others are born into families that simply can't afford to take care of them.

Orphanages need volunteers not only to work with children but to help build or expand their buildings. They have other needs as well. One volunteer ended up cutting (and delicing) the hair of 40 kids. Another went to AIDs clinics in Africa and simply held babies (some studies have shown that receiving love and affection can increase their survival rate). To help children escape the cycle of poverty, some programs at orphanages offer vocational training. They also might provide programs intended to teach life skills and improve self-esteem.

ASK THE EXPERTS

I'd like to help out. Can I volunteer if I'm not trained?

It's not easy. Because of the dangers involved, many organizations that help refugees overseas send only trained professionals. You can, however, help refugees once they arrive in the United States (see pages 190–191) or help one of the many nonprofits that raise money for this cause (see pages 30–31). Good examples are the International Rescue Committee (**www.theirc.org**), World Relief (**www.wr.org**), and World Vision (**www.wvi.org**).

How can I find out how to link up with an orphanage overseas?

You can find information for hundreds of international orphanages—and their volunteer needs—at **www.orphanages.org**. If Christian orphanages are your interest, visit **www.mfinder.org/orphanages.htm**.

My heart aches to do something for those overseas kids, but I'm not ready to travel abroad. Can I do something from here?

Sure! The United Nations Children's Fund (UNICEF) helps worldwide governments, communities, and families care for children who are plagued by poverty, illness, illiteracy, and other crises. If you're looking for a one-time volunteer opportunity, consider organizing a Trick or Treat for UNICEF event in your community. This 50-year-old American tradition, famous for its orange collection boxes, not only raises money and awareness for UNICEF but is often a child's first introduction to compassion, philanthropy, and the reality of the blessings of living in the United States. For one-time or ongoing opportunities, local UNICEF offices throughout the country need help with basic office and administrative duties (see page 40). For more information visit **www.unicefusa.org** or call 800-367-5437.

economic development

Money makes the world go 'round

If you're an established professional in the business world—or even a newcomer—consider donating some time to building businesses abroad. Volunteers present creative solutions to complex problems and plant seeds for long-term international cooperation and business relationships. They also return home with new business ideas and an appreciation for other cultures.

Private businesses and nonprofit organizations need help with money management, fund-raising, business planning, marketing, and just about any other business skill you can think of. But there's still much more to be done. For example, one retired business owner helped women living in a squatters camp in Zimbabwe with small entrepreneurial projects.

As a volunteer for ACDI/VOCA, Patti Carpenter, (center, above) a fashion designer from New York, traveled to Bolivia to work with members of ComArt, a nonprofit association of artisans. Richard Kurtz, another ACDI/VOCA volunteer (middle, right) a marketing consultant from New York, inspects solar-dried tomatoes for quality with Armenian farmers interested in exporting sun-dried products.

ASK THE EXPERTS

How do I get started volunteering in economic development?

Why not try ACDI/VOCA (formerly Agricultural Cooperative Development International (ACDI) and Volunteers in Overseas Cooperative Assistance (VOCA), an international development organization that sends volunteer consultants overseas on short-term technical assignments. All you need are the right skills and the time to spare. ACDI/VOCA volunteers typically are mid-career and senior professionals in their respective fields. To donate two to four weeks of your time, visit **www.volunteeroverseas.com** or **www.acdivoca.org**, contact its headquarters at 800-929-8622, or e-mail volunteer@acdivoca.org. Also, a number of service clubs have international volunteering opportunities, including the Rotary Club (see page 192).

I feel a little overqualified to be working with individual entrepreneurs. Is there anything a little more ambitious I can take on?

Don't underestimate the good that can be done—and the satisfaction that can be gained—through small-scale projects. On the other hand, if you've got real expertise, consider signing up with the Financial Services Volunteer Corps (**www.fsvc.org**)—an opportunity for business executives only. Its volunteers help countries build the infrastructure behind the government and economy. Volunteers travel for one to two weeks at a time and meet with high-level government and banking executives.

Are there any groups that help women-owned businesses abroad?

A variety of programs help women entrepreneurs by teaching them bookkeeping skills, securing credit for their businesses, and helping them find new ways to sell their products. For example, the American Jewish World Service (AJWS) helps poor women entrepreneurs in Peru (**www.ajws.org** or 212-273-1637).

abroad at home

Human rights, especially

In 2001, the U.S. hosted nearly a half million refugees and asylum seekers from around the world. As they arrived here, these weary travelers—often with little more than the clothes on their backs—were assigned to different cities throughout the country.

As they arrive at their assigned destination, refugees and others are helped by local nonprofits to get settled in their new surroundings. That's where the volunteers come in: These organizations need sponsors to care for refugees. What does a sponsor do? Everything from helping the new residents find housing or jobs, raising (or donating) money for the first month's rent, taking them shopping for clothing, or guiding them through the red tape if they sign up for public aid. Does this sound overwhelming? Don't panic. The organization that you sign up through has resources (both financial and informational) to help. In other words, you won't be expected to figure it all out yourself.

Volunteers can give refugees, like those arriving at McGuire Air Force Base from war-torn Kosovo in 1999, encouragement and help with the long process of settling in a new country.

Maybe you're concerned about the language barrier, since many of these displaced folks don't speak English. Bilingual caseworkers are also available to help you cross any language barrier.

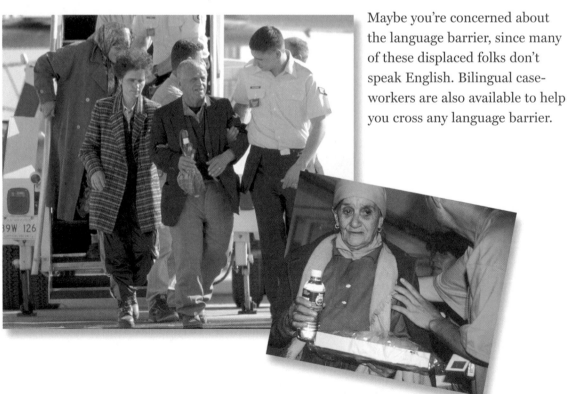

190

ASK THE EXPERTS

I don't have the time to sign on as a sponsor for refugees. Aren't there other ways I can help?

Yes. You can offer to tutor new arrivals in English or simply offer your friendship. Refugees that make it to the United States are often the bravest and most resourceful people you'll ever meet, and helping them find their footing here can go a long way toward making their new lives successful and happy. If you know any refugees, you can approach them directly; if not, contact your local refugee organization and ask for a refugee family to befriend. You might invite them over for tea or a barbeque or take them to a baseball game.

My heart goes out to these people, but I'm not sure I'm ready to work with them directly. Are there any other ways to help?

Consider throwing a shower before a new family arrives in your area. By pooling together with friends, family, or people from work or your house of worship, you can gather goods or cash to help with household items, clothing, or nonperishable food items.

How do I get started helping refugees in the United States?

A number of organizations—mostly churches—help international immigrants get settled. Sponsorship is usually the province of the entire church community instead of one individual or family. Church World Service (**www.churchworldservice.org** 888-297-1516) and Episcopal Migration Ministries (**www.episcopal church.org/emm/**) are just two of the organizations that will tell you how to get involved.

now what do I do?

Answers to common questions

What happens if I get sick while I'm overseas?

Before you go, check with your health insurance provider—many will not cover the cost of your medical care if you are out of the country. If this is the case, consider buying travel insurance before you go. Carriers include CMI Insurance Specialists (**www.studyabroadinsurance.com**) and International Student Insurance (**www.InternationalStudentInsurance.com**).

Can I volunteer abroad through my local Rotary club?

Yes. Whether you want to build clean water wells in Nigeria or help with the Rotary Club's main project—working with the World Health Organization to eradicate polio by the year 2005—the club's international presence makes it easy to volunteer overseas. Contact your local club or **www.rotary.org** for more information on getting involved or securing funding for your own project. If you have a specific business or technical skill, consider signing up for the Rotary Volunteer Corps. In this program, volunteers skilled at everything from dentistry to farming to engineering have volunteered at overseas clinics, improved food quality in underdeveloped nations, and built sewer systems. The possibilities are endless.

What kind of shots will I need if I volunteer overseas? Where do I get them?

It depends on where you go. Some places, like Italy, only require a tetanus shot—you can get that from your regular doctor. But if you need, say, a typhoid shot for going to Cambodia, you might have to go to a special clinic affiliated with your local hospital or medical college. Contact your local health department or the Centers for Disease Control at 888-232-3228 or **www.cdc.gov** for details.

Are there any international volunteering opportunities if I'm disabled?

Indeed there are. The goal of Mobility International USA (click **www.miusa.org** or e-mail clearinghouse@miusa.org) is to help the disabled find and participate in international volunteering opportunities, including disability issues, gender issues, human rights, and other consciousness-raising activities.

Will I need a passport or a visa to volunteer overseas?

You will definitely need a passport, and possibly a visa. Contact your local post office or visit **www.usps.gov** for more information. The U.S. Department of State Web site (**www.state.gov**) not only provides information on passports and visas but gives travel warnings and information on other concerns for international travelers.

Now where do I go?!

CONTACTS

Volunteer Abroad
www.volunteerabroad.com

Peace Corps
www.peacecorps.org
800-424-8580

Volunteer International
www.volunteerinternational.org

Global Volunteers
800-487-1074
www.globalvolunteers.org
Global Volunteers seeks to establish a foundation for peace through mutual international understanding.

Cross Cultural Solutions
www.crossculturalsolutions.org
800-380-4777/914-632-0022
Cross Cultural Solutions is like a mini Peace Corps—it sends volunteers to China, Ghana, India, Peru, and Russia to staff both short-term and long-term volunteer work programs. It targets several areas, such as education (including special education), English language skills, environmental conservation, research assistance, computer training, arts and recreation, and literacy.

Amizade
888-973-4443
www.amizade.org
e-mail: volunteer@amizade.org
Volunteer vacations such as helping to renovate schools in the Himalayas. Amizade is Portuguese for friendship.

BOOKS

So You Want to Join the Peace Corps: What to Know Before You Go
By Dillon Banerjee

Alternatives to the Peace Corps: A Directory of Third World and U.S. Volunteer Opportunities (9th Edition)
By Joan Powell

The Back Door Guide to Short-Term Job Adventures: Internships, Extraordinary Experiences, Seasonal Jobs, Volunteering, Work Abroad
By Michael Landes

How to Live Your Dream of Volunteering Overseas
By Joseph Collins, Stefano Dezerega, Zahara Heckscher, and Anna Lappe

Kibbutz Volunteer (7th Edition)
By Victoria Pybus

11

Your own volunteer project

The best fund-raisers draw
not only money but awareness
for the cause.

who needs what?

Identify the problem

There is a problem and you want to help fix it. Good for you! But what exactly should you do when the problem doesn't fall into a ready-made volunteer niche? You can start your own volunteer project. Yes, you really can. Just take a deep breath and start by taking small steps.

The first step is identifying the need. Sometimes that's easy: Your local high school band needs new uniforms, the library needs a new roof, you want to create a town history, or you want to clean up the local river. Problems like these are pretty straightforward. But what if a factory shut down in your community and caused a rise in unemployment? People need help finding job counseling, applying for federal aid, getting low-cost food, paying their bills, and more. What can you do to help?

Are you a history buff? Gather your town's memorabilia and turn it into a history exhibit to show to the local schools.

That question takes you to the next step—doing a bit of research. You don't want to reinvent the wheel, so ask around and see if there's a project already under way that is trying to help solve the same or similar problem. If it's a simple one-time need that requires fixing, check around and see how a similar problem was handled in the past.

Complex social needs, such as shelter for the homeless or food for the hungry, are usually already being worked on by local or national volunteer organizations. But these groups would be more than happy to entertain a new idea or solution you may have. Your idea for a volunteer project may supplement theirs, and they may be able to help get yours started.

Questions to Ask

1. What exactly is the need or problem?

2. Who would be served by meeting this need?

3. What do they have to say about the need?

4. How long has this need gone unmet?

5. What other volunteering is going on in light of this need?

6. Is there a nonprofit organization at work on this problem?

7. What has been done in the past to help with this problem?

8. Would this need be solved mostly by money, goods, or services?

9. Who could give you advice and help in solving this problem?

10. How much time do you want to spend on fixing this need?

11. Is your family committed to helping you while you help others?

12. What are the consequences of not meeting this need?

13. What obstacles might prevent you from fixing this problem?

What's Really Needed?

Before you do anything, talk with the people whose need you are trying to meet. For example, if the problem you've identified is old band uniforms, check with the band students and make sure they really want new ones. You may be surprised to learn that they think a much bigger problem is out-of-date sheet music. In other words, check your own prejudices at the door and make sure that the need you're trying to address really exists.

building a consensus

Networking is vital

You've identified the problem and you've talked with those who need help. Great. Now what?! Gather a group of like-minded souls to pitch in. There is strength in numbers, because there are then more skills to be used, more time to be lent, more ideas to be garnered, and more talent to be tapped. When it comes to volunteers, more is more.

How will you find that group of people who are interested in your project? The most obvious way is to go to those who need the help. Next, go to those who are affiliated with the project. In the band uniform example, you would want to build a network of interested students, parents, school administrators, music teachers, and sports teams.

How do you do this? Simple: Create a forum for discussion. Find a place (most likely your home or an empty room at the local high school or library) and set a time. Give a rough title to your project and then put the meeting information on a flyer and distribute it to those you think might like the idea. You can cull your volunteers from those who show up or express interest.

Many volunteer projects also grow out of networks based on a shared affiliation, such as a religious group or a garden club. So take a deep breath and appeal to the members of your various groups and ask for help. Chances are they will be glad to lend a hand.

Finally, get the backing of a nonprofit organization. For more on this see page 204. These days it's vital to have a nonprofit organization behind you. It instantly establishes credibility, which helps tremendously in fund-raising.

ASK THE EXPERTS

I want to raise money to send my Girl Scout troop on a camping trip. How do I find people to help me with this?

First of all, make sure there is a consensus about this trip. Do most of the girls want to go? Do their parents support the trip too? Next check to see how funds were raised in the past. Then create a network of core volunteers who have the most to gain from your project, namely the girls and their parents

I want to do something about the uncared-for stray animals in our neighborhood. How do I find out if my neighbors are as concerned as I am?

You can call your neighbors and simply ask how they feel about the issue. Or you can write your thoughts out in a letter and mail it to your neighbors and see who responds. Once you've found interested neighbors, you can proceed with a plan to address the problem.

Money-saving Tips

To maximize your efforts, volunteer projects need to be thrifty. Here are some ways to conserve money while you go about raising it.

1. Don't rent space. Ask if you can use someone's home for meetings. If you need space to store things, ask your church, temple, or school whether they have any spare storage space available.

2. Don't spend money on printed stationery. Just use your computer to create it instead.

3. If you can, find a volunteer to create a Web site about your project. This will give the project instant credibility and visibility.

4. Get a nonprofit sponsoring organization behind you to help you out with logistics. Ask your local Kiwanis club (see page 52) or Jaycees (see page 51) to act as your sponsor and to help lend a hand. Also, you can use their nonprofit status to solicit funding.

5. Don't buy stuff. For example, say you need desks and chairs for your project. Put an ad in the local paper asking for donations. Chances are there may be someone willing to donate what you need—for a good cause, of course.

making it happen

Once you've identified the need and gathered a group of like-minded people, it's time to take a leap of faith. Turn your idea over to the group. The idea has to survive a group critique if it's going to fly, and people need to feel some degree of ownership if they're going to remain committed.

You may find that your idea gets completely trounced in favor of something else that has more of a consensus. Consider it democracy in action, and don't take it personally. Maybe your idea passes muster but needs some tweaking. Either way, you want agreement on the basic need as well as the solution.

Once an idea has been approved, be sure to hammer out the details. You need to come up with a name for your project and

perhaps a logo. But don't let that distract you from more important things—a mission statement and the choice of a leader.

A **mission statement** is simply a statement of purpose. It defines your goals, who will be served by them, and how those goals will be met. This is important because it's easy for volunteer projects to get off target and pulled in different directions. A good mission statement simplifies decisions about what new projects, if any, to take on.

Finally, a leader a must come forward. In many groups, a leader simply emerges. This is the person who can see a bit ahead of the pack and set parameters as well as inspire others to do their part. The leader is not necessarily the person who called the first meeting; it's the person who can make it happen, either because he has a lot of contacts or expertise in the area or because he simply has the time and the passion to do it. If you've never led a group before, being a volunteer project leader is a terrific growth experience, so don't be afraid to step up to the plate. (For more on leadership, see pages 28–29.)

STEP BY STEP

How to write a mission statement

1. State the need and write it down as succinctly as possible.

2. List the people who will be helped by it, and how.

3. State the overall goal of the project. Be specific.

4. State how this goal will be met. If it is fund-raising, explain what type of fund-raising it will be.

5. Make the writing inviting. The mission statement is often the reason people get behind a project.

Foundation for Family Unity Inc.

Mission Statement

We, the Foundation for Family Unity Committee, see as our mission the need to create, sponsor and or/coordinate learning opportunities for parents and their children in the Katonah Lewisboro School District. The opportunities include, but are not limited to:

1. Opportunities for discovering more about issues in parenting and family life, including such topics as communication skills, alcohol and drug abuse prevention, building self-esteem, etc.

2. Opportunities for communication and networking between and among parents and their children.

Implied in these opportunities is the general belief that as we become more effective parents, we can better teach our children to resist negative temptations when growing up and help them achieve their potential as productive and positive adults.

This sample is based on Family University, the Foundation for Family Unity, a nonprofit in Cross River, New York.

finding funding

Getting goods, money, and space

If you think about it, volunteer projects are the wiring that connects people—with time, money, goods, or skills—to unmet community needs. The goal is to make the transmission of it all as glitch-free as possible and, if possible, to raise awareness of the need itself. The best fund-raisers raise not only money but awareness for the cause.

When starting out, volunteer projects need **seed money**—start-up money to get your volunteer project off the ground with incidentals like flyers or the rental space for initial meetings. You can request seed money from a number of nonprofit organizations. For example, if your project is to help the school, the Board of Education (see page 126) or the PTO or PTA (see page 124) may give some money to help out. Or you can ask for seed money from local for-profit businesses, which are usually glad for the goodwill their help generates. (If your project is to help a nonprofit organization, such as a school or religious organization, its donation may be tax-deductible.) If your project is a big one, you can also consider applying for a grant (see page 206).

There are lots of tried-and-true ways to raise money for volunteer projects, and creative fund-raisers are always looking for more. Bake sales, car washes, charity cocktail parties, auctions, and raffles are all common. Another very powerful way to raise funds is to network through your family, friends, and neighbors. People with lots of connections are often the ideal fund-raisers.

Many volunteer groups depend on people donating out of the goodness of their heart. But if possible, it's always good to give something back. That something can be a plateful of homemade cookies or a simple thank-you letter.

Fund-Raising Know How

First, figure out how much money needs to be raised. Then decide on the type of fund-raiser to have. Aside from the traditional bake sale or car wash, here are some other ideas.

- **Product sales** This is the most popular fund-raising technique, because well-run sales can be the most lucrative. (See **www.afrds.org** for more information.)

   In **direct selling**, an organization buys an inventory of products (ranging from candy to long-distance phone services) for volunteers to sell. **Order taking** means that buyers order products from a brochure, and the fund-raising group sends in all order forms to be filled. Products are then either picked up by buyers or delivered by volunteers.

- **Recycling** Raise money and help the environment by recycling items. For example, you could collect discarded items that can be recycled and turn them in for a fee. Or you could collect empty laser and inkjet printer cartridges or used cell phones from the community and redeem them with the Funding Factory for playground equipment, computers, and sports equipment. For more information, visit **www.fundingfactory.com**.

- **Collecting box tops** General Mills cereal box tops can be redeemed for up to $10,000 cash. To learn more, click on **www.boxtops4education.com**.

- **Scrip** Used like cash in stores, scrip is like a gift certificate, and part of the proceeds flow back to a school for which funds are being raised. (A number of national companies have signed on to scrip programs.) For example, buy a $25 Barnes & Noble scrip and 8% (or $2) will be donated to your school. To learn more, visit **www.nationalscripcenter.com**.

nonprofit partners

Finding a sponsor to help
grow your project

Here's the good news: Your project is really taking off! You reached your fund-raising goal and even have some left over—and now you want to continue the effort for a few more years. But unless you've got sponsorship or backing from a nonprofit organization, the not-so-good news is that you'll have to pay taxes on any leftover money you don't spend or can't expense. Moreover, the money people contributed toward your cause can't be deducted on their tax returns. So if you have any intention of keeping your volunteer project going for the long term, you might want to consider joining up with an established nonprofit organization and asking them to be your **fiscal agent,** or money partner. In a sense, they act as your tax-exempt broker. And because they are nonprofit—with a 501(c)(3) tax-exempt certification—you can also use them when applying for grant money. (Remember, only nonprofits can receive most grant money.)

Some nonprofits charge a fee to act as your fiscal agent. It covers the administrative costs of being your agent, and is usually 3 to 10% of whatever funding you receive. As you progress, you may find that you need more from your nonprofit sponsor—for example, office space, equipment, or help from their administrative staff. That kind of relationship is called a **partial association,** and the percentage of fees often is higher.

Another option is to become a local chapter of a national charity that works toward furthering the same cause that you do. If there's no local chapter in your area, you can offer to start one and then bring your project on board.

STEP BY STEP

Starting your own nonprofit

An alternative to working with a nonprofit partner is starting your own nonprofit. It makes sense if you plan to raise more than $25,000, or if you think your project will continue indefinitely. Because the process varies from state to state, go over your state's requirements with a lawyer who specializes in nonprofit law. In general, you will need to:

1. Meet with your volunteer group and decide exactly what type of work your organization will be doing and who will be in charge of the various functions.

2. File the Non-stock Certificate of Incorporation, a form stating that the money the nonprofit makes will not be paid out to shareholders as in a public for-profit business.

3. Prepare and file the Articles of Incorporation, a form that states the name of your nonprofit and the nature of its work and lists the names of the officers. Specifics on how your nonprofit will operate are then listed in the bylaws.

4. File for your federal 501(c)(3) nonprofit tax exemption.

5. If you plan on doing a lot of mailings, file for your federal nonprofit mailing permit, which allows you to mail items at a special reduced rate.

6. Set up a corporate account at your local bank.

7. Create a logo. This will help you get instant recognition when people see your mailings and signs.

8. Get printed stationery bearing your logo.

9. Create a Web page, which will help establish the credibility of your nonprofit. Note: Some high-tech firms will donate this service to nonprofits.

10. Determine who will prepare and file future financial statements with the IRS.

A Smart Move

Becoming an official nonprofit can be a bit daunting, because so much paperwork is involved. But if your project is growing by leaps and bounds, becoming an incorporated nonprofit offers some great benefits. First of all, the money your project makes is tax-exempt. And if you secure 501(c)(3) status, you can now solicit tax-deductible contributions and apply for public (federal and state) grant money (see page 206).

Becoming a nonprofit is a big step. While you can apply for the status yourself, it's wise to contact a lawyer to help you on a pro bono basis. Ask your local Bar Association for names of lawyers on its pro bono committee who know about nonprofit regulations. You should also contact a Certified Public Accountant to help you create your budget and file your financial papers. Preliminary approval takes about three to five months.

all about grants

How they work

A grant is an allocation of money for a particular cause or purpose. It can pay for children's soccer equipment, a senior center, or a writer's room and board at a retreat. If you have an idea and need financial help to make it happen, consider getting a grant.

Naturally, there are strings attached. For your project to be eligible for grant money, it must have nonprofit sponsorship (see page 204). It's a tax thing. To keep tax-exempt status, foundations can give grant money only to tax-exempt nonprofit organizations. Individuals can apply for grant money for themselves, but then they have to pay income tax on the grant money.

Okay, so you have a nonprofit sponsor or tax-exempt status. Now what?! How do you go about getting a grant? First you need to research those charitable organizations that have funded projects like yours in the past. (The best place to start is the Foundation Center, which keeps tabs on major donors. Check out its very helpful Web site: **www.fdncenter.org**.) Once you've found a handful of prospective donors, contact them by phone or e-mail to double-check that they fund projects like yours. Then check their guidelines or Web sites to see how they want to be approached. Some foundations want you to write a brief **letter of intent**, describing your project and needs; others want you to fill out a formal **grant application**. Still others want you to write something called a **grant proposal**, a package of paperwork including a cover letter, your goals and needs, a budget, how you'll carry out your project, and other information.

Yes, applying for grant money can be a bit complicated. But once you learn how to do it and have some success, it will open up endless funding possibilities for your project.

Want to start a recreation center in your hometown? A grant can help you get started.

ASK THE EXPERTS

The charity I volunteer for asked me to write a grant proposal for a project I'm involved in. I've never tried it before, so what should I do?

Don't panic. It can be a great learning experience. Plenty of books out there (such as **Barnes & Noble Basics** *Getting a Grant*) can help, but perhaps the best thing to do is take a course in grant writing. Check with your local library to see if they can help you find courses. Also, the Foundation Center (**www.fdncenter.org**) offers courses on grant writing, and some of them are online.

How long does it take to write a grant proposal?

It depends. Some proposals can be done in a day; others may take weeks. Once you identify five to ten potential funders (that alone can take a good two weeks), write a generic grant proposal. (At the same time, solicit letters of support from your mayor, congressperson, or other officials.) Depending on the complexity of your project, your generic proposal may take two to six weeks to write. Next, spend a few days personalizing your grant proposal to each funder. After that, compile any letters of support you've received and finish all your financial paperwork. Once you've submitted your grant proposal, call to make sure the funder received it.

Our volunteer project could really use a grant, but no one has time to write the proposal. Is there such a thing as a freelance grant writer?

Yes. If you have a nonprofit sponsor, a viable project, and money to spend, consider hiring a freelance grant writer to take care of the whole thing or just those parts you can't manage, such as researching likely grant donors or writing the budget or writing the actual proposal itself. Some writers charge by the hour, others by the project. Click to the Foundation Center's Web site (**www.fdncenter.org**) for a listing of grant writers.

follow-through

Measuring success and showing gratitude

Often, everyone in a volunteer project is so focused on the actual project that when goals are finally met, the group disbands and that's the end of it. That's okay. But a smarter way to go is to have one last meeting to talk about the project and discuss what was helpful and what wasn't. In short, measure your accomplishments against your efforts.

If getting together to talk about it seems impossible, draw up a questionnaire and give it out to the volunteers. You want their feedback about this project, because chances are this volunteer project will be resurrected in a few years and it's good to know what worked and what didn't. This is also the time for all the volunteers to be recognized and acknowledged for the work they did. A lot of projects end without this very important gesture. It is extremely important to thank people who helped make the project happen.

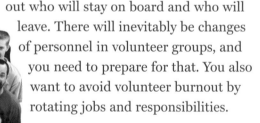

If your project is going to continue, this is the time to figure out who will stay on board and who will leave. There will inevitably be changes of personnel in volunteer groups, and you need to prepare for that. You also want to avoid volunteer burnout by rotating jobs and responsibilities.

STEP BY STEP

The volunteer questionnaire

When volunteers leave the group for any reason, ask them to fill out a form with questions like those below. Feedback from the troops will help your projects run more smoothly.

1. What did you enjoy most about your volunteer experience?

2. Did you feel your role or job was adequately explained to you?

3. What kinds of improvements could be made?

4. Did the project take up more time than you were told?

5. What message would you like to communicate to future volunteers?

6. How did your experience connect you to the mission of the project?

TURNING POINT

I had a strong interest in helping the homeless; in fact, it was almost a calling. One day I got the chance to help out at my church's shelter. From there, I started a small volunteer project to help neighbors with housing trouble in my town. As it grew, I got a great group of people together to help—but I found they kept turning to me to answer every question. (I called it founderitis.) I soon realized that if this effort was going to work, I had to step aside and let the group run it. I split my job into several parts and asked different people to take them over. That helped enormously and made the project that much richer. It also ensured its long-term success.

—Ralph T., Fort Worth, Texas

now what do I do?
Answers to common questions

I spent about $500 of my own money making decorations for our charity ball. I feel funny about asking to be reimbursed for it, but I really can't afford to donate that much. What should I do?

It's okay to ask for money back for expenses incurred in a volunteer project. The project should have a budget in place to handle expense items and reimbursements for them. When possible, get approval for expenses before you start and submit your receipts promptly. (If you can't get reimbursed, get a receipt acknowledging your contribution and talk to your accountant about deducting these expenses on your tax return.)

A group of us created a program to help teenagers with their college applications. How do we know if we actually helped or not?

Ask them. Volunteers who serve a particular group are wise to ask that group if their effort helped. Make a questionnaire and ask the teenagers who participated to fill it out anonymously. Ask them what they thought worked and what didn't. You might be surprised by what you learn, and it will certainly improve your efforts should you continue it in the future.

A local charity wants to fund our entire project, but I'm worried that it may want to make changes. Is that possible?

Yes, it is. But consider this: How long do you want to stay with this project? Even if you are available for several years, remember that this community need may outlive your desire or ability to serve. Getting your project connected to a local funding source may be the best way to ensure it keeps meeting needs long after you've moved on to other projects, even if it means accepting some project changes requested by the charity.

I'm on the board of my local hospital to help raise money. Nothing seems to work. Is there any outside help in the volunteer field I can call?

Yes. You can contact the Association of Fund-raising Professionals (AFP). They have 25,000 members with chapters in every state and many foreign countries. They will have a list of consultants who can help you. You can contact them at **www.afpnet.org**.

How do I organize our project so it goes smoothly?

Create a calendar and divide up key tasks for each month and assign people to do them. Here's an example.

April

- Assign jobs. (president)
- Establish time line. (president)
- Get input from schools. (PTO president and school principal) (liaisons)
- Focus on topics and speakers. (speakers committee)

August

- Have brochures printed (5,500) along with stickers and 150 posters. (brochure volunteer)
- Contact each school and try to be on the schedule for PTA meetings. (liaisons)
- Prepare articles for newsletters. (publicity volunteer)

Now where do I go?!

CONTACTS

www.altrue.com
Helps you create a Web site for your project. Pay what you can afford.

www.nonprofitlaw.com
Devoted to the nonprofit world.

www.fdncenter.org
The Web site of the Foundation Center, a centralized library with information on foundations and grants.

BOOKS

Starting and Running a Nonprofit Organization
By Joan M. Hummel

The Universal Benefits of Volunteering: A Practical Workbook for Nonprofit Organizations, Volunteers, and Corporations
By Walter P. Pidgeon Jr.

High Impact Philanthropy: How Donors, Boards and Nonprofit Organizations Can Transform Communities
By Alan L. Wendroff and Kay Sprinkel Grace

glossary

501(c)(3) Corporations Charitable organizations that meet certain criteria, and apply to the IRS, can receive a special status based on Internal Revenue Code section 501(c)(3). Because donations made to these organizations are tax-deductible, this status is quite desirable. Not all nonprofits or tax-exempt organizations qualify. For example, political organizations, unions, and social clubs are all nonprofits that are tax-exempt but do not qualify for 501(c)(3) status.

Advocacy Advocacy is the process of influencing public opinion and government policy on crucial issues. Advocacy methods include letter-writing campaigns, meetings with government officials, and demonstrations.

Alumni association Alumni associations are nonprofit organizations that allow former students to network, socialize, and volunteer for a variety of causes. A school, college, or university is the common bond between members.

AmeriCorps A domestic version of the Peace Corps, this network of intense service opportunities was created in 1993 and allows volunteers to tutor and mentor youth, build affordable housing, teach computer skills, clean up parks and streams, and help communities respond to disasters. In exchange for a 10- or 12-month full-time commitment, volunteers receive tuition reimbursement, training, health insurance, and sometimes a modest living allowance.

Arboretum A place where trees, shrubs, and plants are cultivated for scientific and educational purposes.

Army Community Service This organization recruits civilians to help Army soldiers with money management, citizenship preparation, income tax preparation, and other areas of life.

Board of directors A board of directors for a nonprofit is a group of people selected to donate their time to help the organization establish its vision and implement the details.

Botanical garden This is a public garden where almost any type of plant is grown, including trees, shrubs, and flowers.

Business and professional organizations Nonprofits whose missions focus on both networking and community service include chambers of commerce, Lions, Rotary, and Kiwanis clubs.

Catholic Charities This private network of social service organizations helps people in need, regardless of their race, age, or faith. Typical services include disaster relief, elderly services, housing assistance, job training, soup kitchens, prison ministry, and substance-abuse programs.

CBO This stands for community-based organizations, which are local nonprofits formed to address some local charitable purpose.

Charity *See* 501(c)(3).

Citizen Corps Citizen Corps was created by President George W. Bush in January 2002 in response to the country's heightened awareness of the need to prevent and respond to major emergencies. This is a new way to volunteer in your community by participating in councils, supporting local police, and being trained for local disaster relief.

City Cares This nonprofit organization with affiliates in over 30 cities offers a variety of interesting volunteer opportunities with no long-term commitment.

Deductible contributions Only deductions to organizations that qualify as 501(c)(3) corporations by the IRS are eligible for a deduction on Schedule A of form 1040.

Development This is another term for fund-raising.

Docent From the Latin word meaning "to teach." Docents are working in zoos, aquariums, museums, and libraries. They are committed to teaching visitors and helping to bring the institution's subject matter to life. They undergo significant training before they can begin.

Election judge Technically not volunteers (since they are paid modestly for their time), election judges work from dawn until dusk on Election Day to ensure that the voting process runs smoothly.

Emergency Medical Technicians (EMT) *See* Volunteer firefighters.

Foundation Center A clearinghouse for all things related to private foundations and the grants they give out. It has library affiliates across the country and a topflight Web site to help people search for information about grants.

Fund-raising Fund-raising encompasses wide-ranging activities that charities use to raise money. These include dinners, auctions, selling products or services, grant writing, and direct mail solicitation.

Garden clubs Local garden clubs enable people who love gardening to come together to share this passion while channeling this interest into local beautification projects.

Grant This is money that is given (generally in response to a formal written request) to a charity by a governmental entity, foundation, or private donor.

Habitat for Humanity Habitat for Humanity International, with affiliates in 50 states and 70 countries, builds simple, affordable houses for people who need shelter. By pitching in hundreds of hours of "sweat equity" as their down payment, these families (along with other volunteers) work with trained supervisors to construct their new housing.

Hospice Hospice is a way of caring for people in the terminal stage of an illness that provides a more homelike environment and lets family members be on hand day or night with their dying relative. These services are provided in either stand-alone facilities, hospital hospice units, or even in the patient's home.

Independent Living Centers These nonprofit community-based organizations provide a variety of services to the disabled, including help with housing, employment, transportation, and with health, recreational, and social issues. They are not places where the disabled live.

Junior League   One of the oldest women's groups in the country, the Association of Junior Leagues provides high-level volunteering opportunities to women who want to grow in the areas of public speaking, managing, and facilitating as they work to improve their communities.

League of Women Voters   This grassroots citizen organization (made up of women and men) provides voters with information, and engages in advocacy to reform public policy issues like the election process or campaign finance.

Meals on Wheels   These are local independent organizations that prepare and deliver hot meals to the elderly and other homebound people.

Mentor   Mentors are generally adults who agree to guide those less experienced in navigating life's rocky roads. By meeting regularly, mentors become positive role models for young people and others.

Navy-Marine Corps Relief Society   This organization provides emergency financial relief to members of the Navy and the Marines and their families.

Nonprofit   Also known as a not-for-profit entity. This is a generic term for organizations set up for charitable, religious, educational, scientific, literary, or other purposes, rather than for-profit financial ones. Not all nonprofits can have 501(c)(3) status—for example, unions or condominium associations do not qualify.

Not-for-profit   *See* Nonprofit.

Peace Corps   Since 1961 the Peace Corps has been sending volunteers abroad to fight "tyranny, poverty, disease, and war." With the main goal of promoting world peace and friendship in mind, Peace Corps volunteers (who commit to over two full years of service) currently serve in over 70 countries. The assignments fall into the categories of education, business, environment, agriculture, health, and community development.

Points of Light   The Points of Light Foundation was founded in 1990. With its network of 500 volunteer centers, its main purpose is connecting people to volunteer opportunities that address serious social problems.

Public relations   Public relations is the act of increasing public awareness about an organization or person, often through the use of the communications media.

Red Cross   Created in 1863 by Henry Dunant in Europe, the International Committee of the Red Cross was originally founded to form relief societies that train volunteers to help care for those wounded during wartime. These societies (now 177 of them worldwide) provide disaster relief, health and social assistance, and first-aid courses. The American Red Cross is one such society, and it is one of the largest volunteer organizations in the country.

Refugees   These are individuals who flee their native countries in order to escape persecution, war, or natural disasters.

Seed money   This is start-up money to get brand-new volunteer projects off the ground.

Senior Corps   This program encourages Americans 55 and over to volunteer in their communities by assisting their local police departments, serving as tutors and mentors for needy children, and helping homebound seniors keep their independence.

Tax-exempt organization A wide variety of nonprofit organizations are exempt from federal income taxes. These include charities listed in IRS code section 501(c)(3), plus dozens of other entities, including credit unions, nonprofit cemetery companies, and fraternities and sororities.

Tithing The biblical mandate practiced by some Christians and observant Jews to give 10% of their earned income back to their church or synagogue. Some people use this term generically for the regular donations they give to their local house of worship.

Tutor A volunteer who helps another person learn about a particular subject. Sometimes the focus is on assigned homework; sometimes its scope reaches beyond assigned schoolwork.

United Way Founded in 1887 by Denver, Colorado, religious leaders, the United Way partners with local schools, businesses, religious groups and governments to help address a broad spectrum of critical local issues. In 1974 the International United Way was formed, which today serves over 40 countries outside the U.S.

USO United Service Organizations (USO) serve the men and women of the armed forces by giving them a "home away from home." They are usually located at airports, military bases, and in large cities.

Virtual volunteering Virtual volunteering allows busy volunteers to give their time from the comfort of their own home (or anywhere that their notebook computers will take them). Common projects include Web design and mentoring via e-mail.

VITA Volunteer Income Tax Assistance (VITA) programs enable tax preparers to help low-income taxpayers, members of the armed services, and the elderly with their income taxes.

Volunteer center These clearinghouses match volunteers with local community service opportunities. Either stand-alone organizations or part of another nonprofit (like the United Way), volunteer centers vary in size from 1 part-time employee to 40 full-time employees.

Volunteer coordinator The volunteer coordinator is the person within a nonprofit who is responsible for helping volunteers find a good fit within the organization. These people are often full-time employees, although they can also be part-time, or even volunteers themselves.

Volunteer firefighters The majority of this country's firefighters and paramedics (also known as emergency medical technicians, or EMT's) are volunteers. Rigorous training enables volunteers to provide these services to their communities.

YMCA/YWCA/YMHA/YWHA (Young Men's Christian Assoc., Young Women's Christian Assoc., Young Men's Hebrew Assoc., Young Women's Hebrew Assoc.) These organizations (which are independent from one another) are nonprofit community service organizations that meet the health and social service needs of their communities. These groups serve people of all faiths.

index

Y

Z

the author: up close

Hope Egan knows firsthand about the ins and outs of volunteering. Among her many volunteer activities, she's been on the board of directors for the Avenue of the Righteous, secured publicity for Business Executives for Economic Justice, and written and edited copy for St. Clement Church's capital campaign and for the Young Adult Ministry's quarterly newsletter. She is also a certified public accountant and financial planner. She was a coauthor of **Barnes & Noble Basics** *Retiring,* (formerly published as *I Want to Retire, Now What?!*)

Barbara J. Morgan Publisher, Silver Lining Books

Barnes & Noble Basics
Barb Chintz Editorial Director
Leonard Vigliarolo Design Director

Barnes & Noble Basics *Volunteering* ™
Lorraine Iannello Managing Editor
David Propson Editor
Monique Boniol Picture Research
Emily Seese Editorial Assistant
Della R. Mancuso Production Manager

Silver Lining Books would like to thank the following for their help in preparing this book:
Jim and Fran Dowling, Cofounders of the Family University, Cross River, New York; **Ann Rumage Fritschner,** a certified fund-raising and nonprofit consultant, Hendersonville, North Carolina; **Deborah Knupp,** 2001 Volunteer of the Year—Make-A-Wish Foundation of Northern Illinois; **Mark Laboe,** Executive Director, Amate House, Chicago, Illinois; **Paul Propson,** Director, the Michigan Neighborhood AmeriCorps Program, Ann Arbor, Michigan; **Bart Tyler** and **Polly Goodwin,** of the Katonah Community Center, Katonah, New York; **Donna Walsh,** member, Board of Education, Katonah-Lewisboro, New York

Photo Credits
ACDI/VOCA: 188; **The American Red Cross:** 8, 100; **The Association of Junior League International:** 54; **Best Buddies International:** 112; **Jake** and **Sarah Rose Chintz:** 88; **Corbis:** AFP/Corbis 7, Bob Krist/Corbis 49, Robert Llewellyn/Corbis 105, Larry Williams/Corbis 121, Bill Varie/Corbis 115; **Corbis:** 148, 154; **Cross-Cultural Solutions:** 180; **Dawid Cymerman:** 83, 90; **Digital Vision/Getty Images:** 195; **Doctors of the World-USA:** 184, 185; **Eyewire/Getty Images:** 141, 144; **McGuire AFB/ Gary Ell:** 190; **Goodwill Industries International, Inc.:** 19; **Habitat for Humanity International:** Joo Cho 98, Mikel Flamm 175, Kim MacDonald 178; **The Image Bank/Getty Images:** 32; **Keep America Beautiful, Inc.:** Cover, 67, 170; **Kiwanis International:** 12, 53; **Lions Clubs International:** 84, 186; **Make-A-Wish Foundation® of America:** 111; **Melanie Pack:** 128; **Robert Milazzo:** 16, 50, 96, 197; **National Wildlife Federation:** 166; **Navy-Marine Corps Relief Society:** 62; **PhotoDisc Collection/Getty Images:** 1, Ryan McVay/Getty Images 132, **The Ocean Conservancy:** 159, 168; **USDA-NRCS:** 162; **VolunteerMatch:** 10; **Young Audiences, Inc.:** Kristen Peterson 134